Set it on Fire

THE ART OF INNOVATION

AVAIL

The ART of LEADERSHIP

Published by AVAIL

Cover design by Sara Young
Cover photo by: Andrew van Tilborgh

ISBN: 978-1-960678-22-5 1 2 3 4 5 6 7 8 9 10

Printed in the United States of America

WHAT PEOPLE ARE SAYING ABOUT *SET IT ON FIRE*

Set It On Fire: The Art of Innovation is Natalie Born's field guide to innovation and leadership that will change any leader's mindset and vision for the future. Natalie encourages the reader to not only get out of the box but to break it and set it on fire! She is a disruptor in her life, and in *Set it On Fire,* she gives practical examples from her deep well of experience to guide the reader on a journey to unlock, advance, and break free from good patterns to make way for great patterns. Leaders set vision, and with great candor, Natalie empowers the reader with solid principles that will either elevate their leadership or make great new leaders out of those who desire to lead. Every person who would like to up their game should read this practical guide!

—Bob Hasson CEO HPCI

Cohost, Exploring the Marketplace *podcast with Shawn Bolz*

Author of Shortcuts, Wired to Hear, *and* Business of Honor

Disrupting yourself is one of the hardest things to do for any organization, yet that's what innovation demands in our complex, fast-paced world. From the heart and based on years of experience, Natalie Born details how innovation really works from behind the scenes. Lucid, practical, and down-to-earth, *Set It On Fire* will challenge your assumptions and help teams break free to set their own fires.

—Jim Kalbach, Chief Evangelist at Mural

Author of The JTBD Playbook *and* Mapping Experiences

Innovation is not an idea, a notion, or a concept. It is an arduous practice that requires perseverance, courage, creativity, and grit. Natalie Born is a true change-maker, so if you're keen on road-tested innovation frameworks and the leadership mindset to mobilize them, this excellent book is for you.

—Sunni Brown
Social Entrepreneur and Best-Selling Author

For Aaron:
Your support has been my strong foundation.
I couldn't do it without you.

For Lily and Gabby:
You inspire me to keep dreaming, learning, and growing.

CONTENTS

FOREWORD

When I was twenty-five years old, I came to the United States with $350 to my name. I wouldn't have believed you if you had told me that down the road, I would publish three best-selling books, experience a company expanding from two hundred to twenty thousand people in a matter of months, cofound a company that empowers marketers to drive revenue impact with account-based marketing, and accomplish so much more.

Hearing others summarize their journeys like I just did use to overwhelm me. How do some people get from point A to point B, even if the odds seem to be stacked against them? In my case, it's because I had people like Natalie Born in my corner—people who have taken the time to fully understand the framework of what it means to be a leader (spoiler alert: Yes, that includes you!) and have gone the extra mile to lend a helping hand and guide others through that process.

I first met Natalie in 2020 through a mutual friend, Amy Balog. If you've also had the privilege of meeting Natalie, you'll know that her contagious positivity is something she carries through both her personal and professional lives. Every task, obstacle, and relationship she encounters is treated with equal enthusiasm, care, and genuine interest. Leaders surround themselves with people who push them to be the best versions of themselves, and Natalie does that as she galvanizes her audiences to press past the limits, the boxes, and the boundaries they have placed themselves in.

If you've ever had an idea you want to develop—in any capacity—this book should be at the top of your list of resources to seek out. Innovation can be intimidating on many levels, but Natalie has a way of unleashing potential in others, and I know this book will do just that for so many fortunate readers. I've recommended her to colleagues, friends, and family for a variety of reasons.

Regardless of what journey you're on or what stage you're at in that journey, her wisdom and experiences will provide the necessary guidance you need, just like they have for me and fellow leaders I'm surrounded by. Natalie has been a consistent source of inspiration for all who follow her and a powerful figure to have in my leadership community because here's the bottom line. Without a community, you are simply a commodity.

While there are many resources out there for both emerging and existing leaders, Natalie stands out. She has a uniquely diversified resume and portfolio—in terms of both industry and geography. She's worked with organizations such as CareerBuilder, First Data, IHG, and ADP, leading major initiatives in over eighteen countries. Today, she's an innovation facilitator, consultant, author, and keynote speaker and hosts the Innovation Meets Leadership podcast. The lessons, tools, frameworks, and questions she's developed for this book have come through her extensive experiences. I have no doubt that you will be a transformed leader after reading this book.

As a leader and entrepreneur, I know how crucial it is for both companies and individuals to have the correct tools to achieve their goals. Natalie's book holds every one of those tools. She'll teach you how to build a strong foundation, ensure your company culture is one that cultivates innovation, position your product and create a go-to-market strategy, and so much more.

There are many things I've learned from Natalie, but the one that stands out most is the value of applying yourself. You can have all the knowledge in the world, but if you don't take the time to develop the necessary skills to most effectively utilize that knowledge, you're wasting your potential.

In summary, when I see successful people, I think of one thing common to all. They are intentional, which is why I always say to myself—and now to you—that being intentional is more important than being brilliant.

This book is about becoming an intentional leader. Now it is your turn to become the leader you always wanted to be.

Sangram Vajre

SANGRAM VAJRE

Wall Street Journal and *USA Today* Best-Selling Author

Co-founder at GTM Partners, Terminus,

and Host of Peak Community

ACKNOWLEDGMENTS

Aaron Born—Thank you for encouraging me to push past my own limits, inspiring me to dream, and supporting me along the way. It's worth saying twice: I couldn't do it without you.

Ron and Doris Hayman—Mom, you were the first female entrepreneur I ever witnessed, showing that women could break through all types of ceilings in business. Dad, I am grateful to you for moving our family away from a bad neighborhood in Philly to Georgia to give us a better life and better opportunities. I'm amazed by all that your nonprofit, I HONOR USA, has done to make a difference in the lives of military men and women serving all over the world.

Lily, thank you so much for your hand-drawn sketches that appear throughout many of these pages. You have so much talent at age thirteen, and I am proud to be your mom. I hope that you will help me with my next book!

THE INNOVATOR'S PLAYBOOK

—A SPECIAL BONUS FROM NATALIE

Now that you have your copy of *Set It On Fire: The Art of Innovation*, you are on your way to creating a culture that unlocks innovation! Plus, you now have a field guide to building innovative teams.

You'll also receive bonus material I created to add to your toolkit. This includes downloads and frameworks all in one place.

When it comes to innovation, I encourage you to get the playbook. You don't have to figure it out on your own. When you finish this book, you'll be armed with what you need to know to create more innovative teams and launch products that matter in the market.

www.SetItOnFire.co

Remember: Don't just get out of the box. Break the box, and set it on fire. Let's go transform something!

All the best,

NATALIE BORN

INTRODUCTION

WHERE'S THE PLAYBOOK?

In ninth grade, I had huge dreams of studying genetics. I was enthralled with my biology class and couldn't wait to learn. I was fully engaged in understanding how things like eye color, hair color, and even disease could be passed down from parents to children. I was all in, and that led me to sign up for AP (Advanced Placement) Biology in my eleventh-grade year. I just knew I was going to be a world-famous geneticist.

Then my dream took a very quick and sharp turn. Everyone in the class, minus me, had taken AP Chemistry the semester before with the same teacher. I was lost and didn't have a clue what was going on. She kept referring to concepts that the students had learned the previous semester. That, for sure, took a toll. I slowly stopped paying attention because I was lost and disengaged. I felt helpless, and keeping up felt impossible. I was slipping into mediocrity.

Out of the kindness of her heart, she allowed me to pass the class because she could see I was trying. It was like everyone had this playbook that I didn't own because I didn't have a seat at the other table. I didn't love chemistry. Why was it the bridge to our class in biology?

Later in life, I felt the same way when I entered the business world. I felt there was a lid over my career. It seemed like people had more knowledge, clarity, and ability to understand some of the business concepts, acumen, and ways of working that were being thrown at them daily. While I had no clue what half of those concepts meant, I would jot them down, go away, and study them on my own. But how did people similar in age to me seem to understand these concepts?

That path led me to go back to school for my Master's in Business Administration with a concentration in International Business. I couldn't articulate why, but in many meeting rooms, I felt that I was at a distinct disadvantage. I wanted to learn and grow as rapidly as I could, but I lacked the exposure I needed to understand some of the basic business concepts that were being thrown around and how to apply them.

Doesn't this story ring true in our lives at times? There's a playbook that people seem to be following, and we just can't figure it out. They must have gone to classes that we didn't attend. They must have studied under a teacher we didn't have. They must play golf with the CEO and his buddies every weekend.

Today, I want to give you a behind-the-scenes look at—a playbook on—innovation from the things I have learned over the years during my time in product development and sales and as an innovation consultant. When I was first getting started in innovation and product development, I had the opportunity to work with teams in over eighteen countries. These methodologies apply in the United States, where I first began to implement them, and in other countries like China, Singapore, Italy, and France. Foundationally, after reading this book, you will have the methodologies that I used to build products from the ground up. Many of those products have gone on to win awards or become patented because these methodologies work!

Before we begin, every leader must ask themselves a few direct questions. Before even launching into innovation, we must believe innovation is possible. Often a lack of belief starts earlier than we'd like to admit.

So, let me ask:

Who told you that you are not innovative?

Who told you that you are not creative?

Was it something someone said to you or something you've been saying to yourself?

On my platform, I call myself a disrupter, and the first person I always want to disrupt is myself and my own limiting way of thinking. We often hold ourselves back by the boxes we put ourselves in. We tell ourselves what we can or cannot do before we have even tried it. Over time, what we can't do is what begins to define us.

So, let's make the question obvious:

Is your way of thinking the lid on your life?

Everyone has innovation, ingenuity, and creativity inside of them, waiting to be released. As we take this journey together, let's see how we can create a culture that unlocks, advances, and disrupts the box people have asked us to live in. It's time to break free!

From working with teams of all types from all over the world, I can assure you that innovation is in you. When you allow yourself to think innovatively, it unleashes limitless possibilities! And once you transform your mindset, you can work toward transforming the mindset of the organization.

There are several core attributes that really drive cultural innovation. These elements speed up innovation and create highways for ideas and creativity to flow. If we begin to shut down or ignore these areas of innovation, it gets exponentially harder to innovate. When idea highways are closed off, innovation becomes nonexistent. Before thinking, *I am not in a seat that innovates*, let me strongly disagree. Every leader must be strong in innovation. It is the leader's role to see around corners and create the future. Innovation affords you the opportunity to do that.

To define innovation, let's think of innovation as the ability to spark something new. It is to do something that has never been done before, to create a new path, to disrupt old ways of thinking. Let this book serve as a guide to where to focus over the next six to twelve months. Create a culture in your organization that may not exist today. So, let's not delay. Let's go transform something!

Chapter 1

STRONG FOUNDATIONS ALWAYS ACCELERATE INNOVATION

"Innovation is the ability to see change as an opportunity—not a threat."

—STEVE JOBS[1]

I got into the elevator and hit the button for the lower level. As I emerge and walked down the hall, it was the first time that I hadn't felt nervous about an interview. It was pure curiosity that drove me to even have the conversation. Normally, when I am going for a new role, I really pitch them hard, put all my cards on the table, and go for bust.

I walked into the meeting with the international product development department and sat down in a small office. I worked upstairs

1 George Baker, Sr., "Council Post: Four Concepts to Drive Innovation in a Time of Crisis," *Forbes*, 21 Aug. 2020, https://www.forbes.com/sites/forbesbusinesscouncil/2020/08/24/four-concepts-to-drive-innovation-in-a-time-of-crisis/?sh=745030e34daa.

as a project manager, but technology was where most of us aspired to be. When I walked in for my interview for a product development manager role, I said, "Here are some international projects I am working on right now, but I have no idea if I would be a good fit for the team." Who says that? It's like saying, "You don't have to hire me unless you want to." I look back at that moment often—and laugh.

I was even more shocked when they called me back later to tell me I had gotten the job. I would never recommend getting a job that way, but I really did stumble into product development out of sheer curiosity, and that curiosity led me to my passion. Working on products was so exciting. It was the thought of taking something formless, empty, and vague—just an idea—and turning it into something useful to improve the way people work or live. It's not creative, working with something that already exists; it's innovative, building something that has never been thought of before. Innovation is pioneering new ground and reaching new heights.

But if you are anything like I am, you don't see yourself as naturally innovative. Despite that factor, I can still remember the call to innovate that came in the middle of a crisis. It was during the 2008 financial crisis, and my company found itself in the middle of layoffs. Actually, the whole world found itself in the middle of layoffs, and most organizations were reeling—trying to stay afloat. The management team was pulling people into rooms and letting them know that they would be receiving a severance package. Good friends and former coworkers were packing up their desks, and as a mid-level manager, I felt helpless. Our CEO brought us together and gave us this mandate:

"We need to create two new innovative products every year." *Wow*, I thought, *we are still reeling from the losses. How are we going to do this?*

In hindsight, the CEO's direction was brilliant.

Innovation Principle: Vision sees beyond circumstance.

When times get tough, people typically look at the problem. Most of the time, we can't inherently fix the problem. Good luck single-handedly fixing the economy. But what can we do? We can create a vision for a future that doesn't exist. This is a core principle of innovation, with or without a crisis. We must give people a vision beyond their current circumstances.

Our vision, mission, values, and goals become the bedrock or fundamental principles on which we build where our company is going and how we will know when we get there.

VISION, MISSION, VALUES, AND GOALS

Anything you build should be on the foundation of your vision, mission, values, and goals. These are your true north. It's not surprising to realize that most people working in an organization cannot articulate their company's vision, mission, values, or goals.

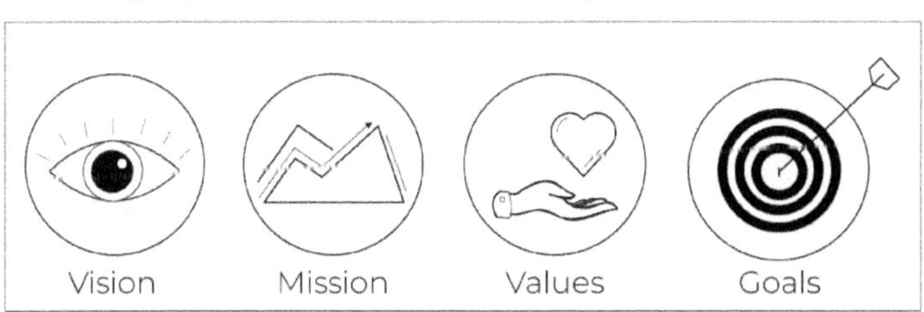

What Makes a Vision?

A vision is a picture of the future that is clear enough in its description that others have an idea of where to go and big enough to inspire others to want to go there. A good vision statement should propel us to think fifteen to twenty years into the future. It should feel aspirational; we know we will have to work hard to achieve it. Your vision creates the future that you want.

Let's take an example from history. On May 25, 1961, United States President John F. Kennedy spoke to Congress, asking for money for the space program. He said, "I believe that this nation should commit itself to achieving the goal, before this decade is out, of landing a man on the moon and returning him safely to earth."[2] That is a clear, compelling, and captivating vision.

Around that same time, another man had a well-defined and enthralling vision as well. On August 28, 1963, Martin Luther King Jr. presented a speech that rocked the nation. It's a speech we still reference today. He called the gathering that day at the Lincoln Memorial in Washington, DC "... the greatest demonstration for freedom in the history of our nation."[3] His "I Have a Dream" speech was a clear ask for equality for all people from the United States government as King described his vision for an integrated and equal America.[4]

That is a clear vision statement. It projects out into the future, and it is something we can all rally around.

---

2 Brian Dunbar, "Excerpt from the 'Special Message to the Congress on Urgent National Needs'," *NASA*, 11 Apr. 2017, https://www.nasa.gov/vision/space/features/jfk_speech_text.html.
3 "Dr. Martin Luther King, Jr.: Freedom. Equality. Justice," *ORTEC*, 13 Jan. 2022, https://ortec.com/en-us/news-more/insights/remembering-dr-martin-luther-king-jr-freedom-equality-justice.
4 "Martin Luther King I Have a Dream Speech," *American Rhetoric*, https://www.americanrhetoric.com/speeches/mlkihaveadream.htm.

Vision statements are powerful when they are:

- Well-written
- Clear
- Memorable
- Concise

A vision is a set of shared beliefs that help us to achieve our goals no matter how impossible they may seem. A vision describes the future that we want to create. Those that read the vision should be inspired to run with it. Your vision should ignite innovation and action in the hearts and minds of those who read it. It should move the team from transactional to transformational.

What Makes a Mission?

If your vision galvanizes your team to plan for the future, your mission explains what's taking place today. It answers questions: *What do we do?* and *Whom do we serve?* It sets and impacts the organization's culture deeply.

Mission statements are powerful when they:

- Push the team toward a common goal.
- Empower the team to act.
- Explain what we do and for whom we do it.

Mission statements can evolve over time to take you closer to your vision. When people are off mission, they create silos, establish turf, and fight for what is best for their team over what is best for the organization. When you establish a clear mission, it helps boats to all row in the same direction.

TED's mission statement, "Spread ideas . . ." is pithy and simple.[5] It is this simplicity that makes it clear to understand if you are winning. Nike's mission statement is also clear: "To bring inspiration and innovation to every athlete* in the world. (*If you have a body, you are an athlete.)"[6]

As you can see, vision and mission are essential to igniting and inspiring your team's forward momentum. These items are your true north, and when you are not around, it tells your team the "what" and "where" of their work.

What Makes Strong Values?

Over time, leaders understand the impact and power of values. Values are the DNA or culture of the organization. If we truly live our values, we will hire and fire by them because values drive performance. Our values become the agreement dictating how we will behave and how our culture will function. Values are actionable. They are things we can do. People can also recognize when we are not living the values.

I once worked for an organization where one of its values was candor. According to the *Merriam-Webster Dictionary*, "Candor . . . refers to straightforward honesty or frankness in speech or expression."[7] So what did that mean for the way we operated? It meant that we didn't need to beat around the bush when giving feedback. We

5 "Our Mission: Spread Ideas, Foster Community and Create Impact," *TED*, https://www.ted.com/about/our-organization.
6 "Our Mission . . . ," *About.nike.com*, https://about.nike.com/en.
7 "Candor Definition & Meaning," *Merriam-Webster*, https://www.merriam-webster.com/dictionary/candor#:~:text=Candor%2C%20related%20to%20the%20adjective,frankness%20in%20speech%20or%20expression.

could be open and honest with our concerns no matter with whom we were speaking. We could cut through the formalities and get to the point. It is actually a beautiful thing in a fast-paced, innovative environment.

Because I saw the value of candor, it became one of my personal values as well. So what happens when you go to an organization that doesn't value candor? You have a really hard time working there. When you communicate with openness and honesty, and people see that as a direct attack or pushback on their personal leadership, it becomes a problem. In your mind, you are being truthful to further the greater good. In their mind, you are opposing their plans and standing in their way. Now, what we have is a clear clash in our values. Values matter because values make or break organizations. Ensuring you have a value fit saves you time, energy, and effort. Organizations become toxic when they hire people who are misaligned with their values.

Living the Values

One of the hardest things to come across is someone with real and raw talent who does not live the organization's expressed values. I had one employee who was merged into my team when I entered into a new role; we will call him Sam. He was incredibly talented, and it was always impressive to see the final product of his work. However, it almost always came late. Sam would frequently miss meetings that he was supposed to lead, and I would be left there, looking at the rest of the team, with no answers. Over time, not exercising any discipline toward Sam became an issue. Other leaders on my team were looking at me thinking, *We show up on time. We turn our work in on time. Why does Sam get a pass?* They were right. Why was everyone else doing the right thing, yet Sam was getting the same reward (his job) for doing the wrong thing?

I sat down with Sam to explain what the organization was looking for in an employee. I laid out our values and explained that accountability and dependability are things we hire and fire for. I gave him a warning. Afterward, I followed up with an email outlining our conversation and the changed behavior I was hoping to see.

A couple of weeks went by, and things were looking up. Slowly, he started to take on more accountability, and he became more dependable. But unfortunately, after a few more weeks passed, things went right back to the way they were. I wrote Sam up for missing key meetings and turning work in late once again. He was such a talented individual, but I could not figure out how to motivate him. After several more write-ups, we reached the final straw.

One morning, I asked Sam to swing by my office. "Sam, tomorrow is a big day for our team," I told him. "We have our team meeting. It starts at 9:00 a.m., and I know that historically, I don't really see you around the office until 10:30 a.m. I need you to be there on time. If you are not there on time, I will be asking you to get a box, pack your things, and leave the office. I am giving you this heads-up because this is your last warning."

I cannot make up what Sam asked me next. "Can you call and wake me up?"

Taken aback, I replied, "No. I am not your mom. But I do hope you can make it on time."

You will not be surprised to find out that Sam was an hour and a half late for our team meeting.

By Monday, I was letting go of one of the most talented team members I had. Why? Because he constantly disregarded our values. It didn't matter that his talent was off the charts. We said we valued accountability and dependability, and he was not pulling his weight in these areas.

I hated to walk him to the door that day, but the team and I had suffered long enough. When you have someone who's misaligned with your values, the whole team suffers, and your company suffers too. So, know what you value, hire what you value, and fire when someone is misaligned to those values.

Setting Company Goals

The more employees you hire, the harder it is to keep everyone on the same page. To really begin setting goals, it's important to look at where you want the company to be in three to five years. Once you feel clear on that, start to walk backward and figure out what you will need to do annually and then quarterly to reach that three- or five-year goal.

For example, if in three years, we want to be number one in our market, we have to ask:

- Where are we now?
    - To answer this question, it may be as simple as a SWOT (strengths, weakness, opportunities, and threats) or competitive analysis. This will even help us understand what is holding us back from getting where we want to go.

- What metrics will we use to measure movement?
    - This could be the number of users on our platform or a key revenue number we desire to hit.
- What capabilities do we need to build or acquire to become number one?
    - This question really helps us set clear goals. If we lack certain core capabilities, we may need to start there before we can build toward our plan.

Making It Plain

Here's an example of a vision that I helped to implement for a team. Everyone received one of these framed so that the vision would always be in front of them. When we have performance reviews or developmental conversations, the vision is always there to help lead us to our true north.

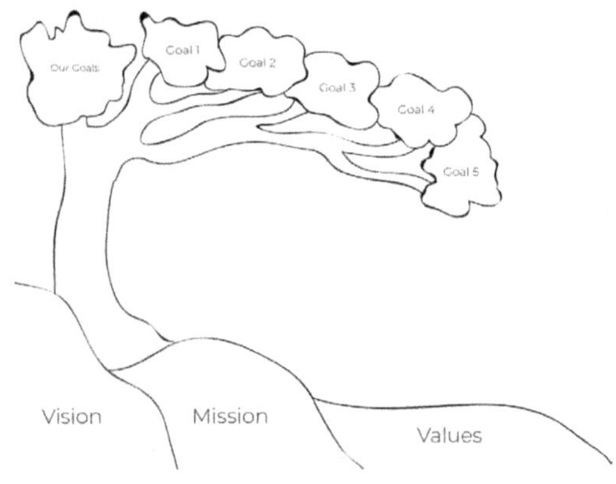

Keeping the Vision Visible

What if every team member had the vision displayed on their desk or in their office? You can't carry the vision of the organization if you don't know what it is. What if we put it front and center visually so that team members could use that vision to make key decisions?

A decision framework is created to ensure that your leadership team and those who report to them can use critical thinking to make key decisions. This framework should look through the lens of the vision, mission, values, and goals and act as rails when decisions are to be made.

Your decision framework should be aligned according to these four areas:

1. **Vision**—What do we hope to achieve in the future?
2. **Mission**—What is our purpose for existing, and what are we doing today?
3. **Company Values**—What are our core principles, and what do we value as an organization?
4. **Our Goal**—What are the BIG goals we are trying to achieve as a company?

So, when there was a call during the 2008 economic crisis to innovate, it was all about vision over circumstance. During this time, I learned the three core roles of the leader and the three core roles of the team.

THE ROLES OF THE LEADER

There are three main things that a leader should provide to their team: vision, resources, and clarity on how to adapt the goals to traverse the changing landscape.

ONE—A Leader Must Set the Vision

A vision functions as true north. It tells people where to aim their cannons and in which direction to plot their course. It's easier to course correct when you assess the destination against the vision. A leader's role is to set the course and the speed at which we are going to travel. The leader guides us to the destination by figuring out what sparks tenacity and motivation within the team.

A leader's role is to get the team really excited about the journey by helping them lock onto the vision. While most team members show up motivated, it's very easy to demotivate them by not properly understanding their skill sets and knowledge, by belittling them, or by being a leader who tells people *what* to do without telling them *why*. There's also something arguably more powerful than motivation, and that is inspiration. So, let's inspire!

TWO—A Leader Must Provide the Resources

There's nothing more demotivating than having a big vision but no resources to accomplish it. Most leaders are moving so fast that they forget to, as Dr. Stephen R. Covey says, "Begin with the End in Mind."[8] Part of the role of a leader is to remove roadblocks preventing the execution of the vision. Resources are not always monetary; sometimes, they come in the form of time or attention. Time in the right rooms and attention from the right people achieve the goals.

Several days or weeks of research could save you years of heartache. Reaching into the unknown can be an exciting and empowering

8 Stephen R. Covey, *The 7 Habits of Highly Effective People* (New York, NY: Simon & Schuster, 2020) 109.

experience, but you must first ensure you've counted the costs and can provide the proper resources, so your team can begin the journey. A leader doesn't have to do this alone. The team is there to help provide perspective and give feedback.

THREE—A Leader Must Adapt the Goals to the Changing Landscape

It's not enough to create a vision and roll it out; we have to look at how the vision is responding to our current landscape. Creating clear and measurable goals will ensure that we are on the right path.

Agility is a superpower today. Not only do we need to be agile with any goals and plans we make, but we also need to be flexible with a vision that can scale up or down with that plan. When the economic winds come, how will we change our planned goals? If we have supply chain issues, how do we pivot our planned goals and create a vision that can withstand the storm? You and your team will be stronger by asking some hard questions before you get in too deep.

THE ROLE OF THE TEAM

A team member is signing up to do three main things in lockstep with the vision that is created: carry the vision, get creative with the resources, and innovate by building what doesn't exist.

ONE—Carry the Vision

A team member must ensure that they understand the vision enough to implement it. It's not enough to know the vision; they must contextualize it to their day-to-day. A team member must carry the vision, reiterate the vision, and make decisions through the lens of the vision. As a team member, it's crucial to keep the vision in front of us at all times. When making key decisions, we have to ask ourselves, *Does this align with the vision?* If not, then reconsider your stance or approach.

TWO—Get Creative with the Resources

While the leader's role is to provide the resources and remove roadblocks, the team's role is to understand the landscape, utilize the resources they have, and get really creative. Regardless of how much we plan, there's no doubt that it'll be necessary to get creative with the resources we have.

A team member should be asking questions: *How can I save time or money without sacrificing quality? How can we do more with less? How can we overdeliver under budget?* When someone treats resources like their own money and is a good steward, leaders trust and want to promote that person to handle more. Ask the hard questions, and find places to be scrappy without sacrificing quality.

THREE—Innovate by Building What Doesn't Exist

This is the hardest part. We need to set our teams up in such a way that they can try new things. Let's help them fail quickly and cheaply, and in that, help them fail forward. We do that by introducing incremental—not big and bold—changes. We test and adjust constantly.

LEADER AND TEAM ROLES

THE LEADER'S ROLE	THE TEAM'S ROLE
Set the vision.	Carry the vision.
Provide the resources.	Get creative with the resources.
Adapt the goals to the changing landscape.	Innovate by building what doesn't exist.

When you have alignment around vision, mission, values, and goals, the way the team makes decisions should feel similar to that of the CEO and founder.

Consider This: *Why do organizations want to hoard decision-making at the top? What if we gave people a framework on how to make important decisions and then gave them freedom within that framework?*

When I look back on some of the projects I was working on at twenty-four and twenty-five years old, I realize that our vision was so articulate that I had clarity in my decision-making ability. I understood my guardrails. I was grounded in what my leaders and the founders wanted and where we were headed. I can remember a few times when I really stepped in it and made a bad call, but most of the time, I was able to run. I had freedom within the framework.

If the leader has to make all of the decisions all the time, that's not leading. That's micromanaging. The leader marks the spot on the map, and it's the team's job to navigate us there.

TAKING ACTION:

- What does it take to become someone who leads with vision?
- What are some ways you can keep the vision in front of your team?
- What less important functions and details could someone else manage, so you can focus on the vision?

FRAMEWORK TOOLS:

- Creating a Vision, Mission, Values, and Goals

Chapter 2

"GET OUT OF MY SANDBOX!" WHY TEAMING IS A LINCHPIN FOR INNOVATION

"In order for collaboration to take place, managers must give up their silos and their perceptions of power."

—KEN BLANCHARD[9]

Let's journey back to when my team was told we had to create two new innovative products each year. We couldn't see the future, but we *could* look at the customers' needs and the trends and become a visionary to predict where the market was going. We basically needed to make a very solid educated guess.

My team worked in the software-as-a-service (SAAS) industry, and two products seemed "easy" enough. We thought, *Let's get our*

9 Kenneth H. Blanchard, Jane Ripley, and Eunice Parisi-Carew, *Collaboration Begins with You: Be a Silo Buster* (Oakland, CA: Berrett-Koehler Publishers, 2015).

best engineers, product developers, marketers, salespeople, customers, and thinkers to the table. Let's roll up our sleeves and go to work. At that time, we already had several ways to surface good ideas. We had business plan competitions, hackathons, executive ideas, competitive analysis, customer visits, and listening sessions.

I personally loved sitting across from customers and letting them tell me what they loved and hated about our products and the competitors' products. In our industry, they would often use one to three of our competitors simultaneously, and I appreciated hearing what was and wasn't working. The beauty is if you have enough of these informal sessions, you really begin to surface patterns. Innovation is simply surfacing and monetizing patterns that we see in daily problems and tensions our customers are trying to solve.

Consider This: *Your customer's problems are your next features and products.*

We have to put in the work to surface customer problems and turn them into viable solutions.

Innovation Principle: Innovation is simply surfacing and monetizing patterns.

While there are several ways to surface innovative ideas in an organization, including contests that I mentioned above, it's an endeavor to not work in silos. We worked across all the different teams. That's what I love about pure innovation. We push our agendas out of the way and ask questions: *What can we build with what we have? What can we create that doesn't exist today?* We frequently took our ideas internal and external to validate them—internal to our teams and external to our customers.

Innovation Principle: Innovation isn't built in silos.

TAKING IDEAS INTERNAL

Once we realize that our teams have surfaced a good idea that has potential, we need to test it. We take ideas internal for collaboration and feasibility. It's important in the early stages of an idea to ask the questions like, *What would need to be true to make this idea work?*

Most organizations work under a culture of "no" or "can't," and it makes it impossible to move good ideas forward. Teams are constantly running into internal roadblocks along the way. Asking the question *What would need to be true?* helps to shift some of this "no" thinking and puts people in more of a collaborative mindset.

Even if we find that our internal teams are more "no" driven, it doesn't mean we should ignore the wisdom they can provide. Our internal teams can help us avoid land mines, and before you think we are talking about technical land mines, we are talking about the landmine of buy-in. Our teams must be brought into the idea or the vision that we are building toward. To do that, they need to be able to share thoughts, concerns, and ideas and bring context to the broader scope of what we are building toward.

Consider This: *Oftentimes, internal teams are defensive because they are not brought in early enough to provide their thoughts and help make key innovation decisions.*

From Resistant Blocker to Supportive Backer

Often, this is where we need to slow down to speed up. By providing teams with enough information to become our thinking partners, we do several things:

1. Let them know their voice matters and makes a difference.
2. Invite them to the table to help us solve the problem.
3. Highlight anything we may be missing.
4. Improve morale by not inventing in silos.

At one point, I worked on an outsourcing project to move items and tasks overseas that our US teams found quite monotonous. My boss asked me to sit down with my peers and bring them up to speed with my plans. I didn't understand why. I was doing my job, and they were doing theirs. They didn't sit down with me and tell me what they are working on, so I thought, *Why should I do that for them?*

What he was asking me to make was a strategic move. One that would help my peers trust me, feel they had a seat at the table with the work that I was doing, and not fear that their jobs were on the chopping block next due to outsourcing. Being immature in my career, I never understood the value of socializing my plans and ideas. However, when we do, it builds trust, and that trust improves morale. That trust also takes a person from *resistant blocker* to *supportive backer*.

Taking ideas internal isn't about making other employees feel good. It's about bringing collaboration to the table as a form of currency. We are showing the team that they are a valuable and important part of our process, and when we do that, it destroys the desire people have to work in silos.

SILOS SUCK RESOURCES

In another instance, I was working on a project that took me to Singapore and China for several weeks. I was shocked to find out that back home in the US, we were all trying to solve the same problem. Imagine that: three teams in three different countries, all trying to build the same product for the same end user. When this happens, we create huge technical debt and waste our organization's resources exponentially.

This, by definition, is a silo: everyone doing their work within their organization and no one talking to the other teams outside of their department. Independent instead of interdependent. My trips to China and Singapore were to share what we were working on and see if there were places of interest where we could collaborate. Build it once versus build it three times. Catching these types of off the rails projects in the organization saves us hundreds of thousands—if not millions—of dollars.

Breaking down silos should be a primary goal for all leaders because silos:

1. Waste talent
2. Waste time
3. Waste money
4. Waste energy and effort
5. Destroy morale
6. Make us feel like it's us vs. them
7. Create confusion for the customer

Many silos are created because it's just faster or easier, but some silos are created because of ego. Like when I was younger, I created a silo because I didn't want anyone in my business area. I wanted to work on it all myself. I never did gel with that team because I didn't invite them in. Silos create barriers for teams, hog resources and knowledge that should be shared, and keep people on the outs that should be at the table.

Consider This: *Your teams are not moving as one because they would rather play in their own sandboxes. It's faster and easier—and they don't experience any resistance.*

Does your culture reward the team working together, or does it reward an every-man-for-himself mentality?

TAKING IDEAS EXTERNAL

When we begin to take the idea external it's to test desirability and to create a customer sense of urgency to buy. Keep in mind that we have not built anything yet. We are talking to customers so that we can surface problems, opportunities, and patterns that are solvable.

As a product development director, I worked with one of my customers on a new product that we wanted to see in the market due to the harsh competitive landscape. We started in sketch format and moved all the way to prototype with her. I had not been in her office for more than two minutes when she blurted out, "I hate this product." I felt all the blood rush to my face because she was calling my baby ugly. I was triggered, but instead of defending the product, I took a deep breath and leaned into the feedback.

I said, "Hit me with all your concerns, and don't leave out any details." There were many clear problems, and after about thirty minutes of notetaking, I looked up at her and said, "Your detailed assessment of what is not working is so comprehensive that I bet you will notice right away if we even make half of these changes. If I commit to making things better over the next three months, will you commit to sticking around long enough to give feedback on the changes? You have helped me to know where we can focus to get better, and that is a gift."

As I left her office that day, I knew we were both on the hook. I was on the hook to deliver, and she was on the hook to provide more feedback. Feedback is a gift. If she hated the product, it would never successfully make it to market. What if she never said anything?

Taking ideas external and really being willing to hear what people have to say will save you time, money, and resources.

Consider This: *If someone is bold enough to tell you something is not working, have the courage to listen and then rapidly grow and develop that idea further based on that feedback.*

Most of us are in the business of solving problems for others, so iterating helps us solve their problems more rapidly. Working across the organization and out in the field gave us the stories that we needed for credibility. If you want to innovate, those around you must sense that you are building the right thing for the right people. Capturing stories as you build drives that credibility. Organizationally speaking, creating a culture of innovation doesn't just happen. Studies show that key attributes give rise to innovation.

PROJECT ARISTOTLE

When we think about teaming over the years, organizations like Google have really set the standard. But as we know, teaming is hard, and ego, incompetency, personality clashes, and unclear direction can get in the way. Google's people analytics team set out to study what makes a great manager, and that project morphed into what makes great and effective team members. They named the project Aristotle based on the quote attributed to him: "The whole is greater than the sum of its parts," and the goal was to answer the question: What makes a team effective at Google?

In their research, the team identified 180 teams from engineering and sales, with a mix of high- and low-performing members to understand the team dynamics. They not only reviewed existing data, including annual employee engagement surveys, but also Google's study on work and life. They conducted hundreds of interviews to understand what drove team effectiveness.

Some of the items they used in their study and asked subjects to agree or disagree with were:

- If they felt safe expressing a divergent opinion from that of their team. (Group Dynamics)
- If they felt they were good at navigating barriers and roadblocks. (Skill Sets)
- If they saw themselves as someone who is reliable at work. (Personality Traits)
- If they were interested in other people's problems. (Emotional Intelligence)[10]

In addition to these questions, demographics like tenure, level, and location were also included. Out of this study, five attributes emerged:

1. Dependability
2. Structure and Clarity
3. Meaning of Work
4. Impact of Work
5. Psychological Safety

10 "Re: Work," *Google*, https://rework.withgoogle.com/print/guides/5721312655835136/.

Dependability

Can we count on you?

In the last chapter, we spent a great deal of time talking about Sam. He was not a dependable team member. As a result, the team not only stopped trusting him, but the team dynamic also began to break down. So, what does it truly mean to be dependable?

Dependability is:

- Doing what you say you are going to do when you say you are going to do it.
- Showing up on time and not leaving early.
- Taking responsibility for your role and going above and beyond to help others if needed.
- Acknowledging our imperfection. We overcommunicate if something has changed, and we are not able to show up in the way we want to.

The people that I really love working with are always underpromising and overdelivering. That's dependability.

Structure and Clarity

Are the goals and roles of the team clear?

I believe it's the leader's job to provide structure and clarity. If the team does not have clarity, it's their job to pursue it until it's found.

Structure and Clarity are:

- Clearly understanding your role and the roles of your peers.
- Clearly understanding how your role fits into the larger ecosystem at your company.

- Understanding the formal and informal ways to get answers to questions and get work done.
- Understanding what is expected of you (and the team), how you (and the team) will be measured, and how to win.
- Having clear performance objectives.

When teams don't have to constantly question how they are doing and if they are secure in these areas, they can move as one to get things done.

Meaning of Work

Are we working on things that matter to us?

Much has changed since the early 1900s; people really want to know if their work has meaning and if it matters. People are no longer going to work just to collect a paycheck. They want to make a difference.

Meaning of Work asks:

- Where am I in Maslow's hierarchy of needs?[11] Am I able to support and care for my family (physiological)? Do I have financial security (safety)? But it doesn't end there.
- Does this role serve a deeper meaning in my life?
- Are we reaching for a purpose—such as an important cause—that is bigger than revenue?
- Are we working on things that matter to us and the world around us?

11 Saul McLeod, "Maslow's Hierarchy of Needs Theory," *Simply Psychology*, 2 Mar. 2023, https://simplypsychology.org/maslow.html.

Meaning matters to the team, and the leader's job is to help people connect their roles and tasks to a larger meaning in the organization. That meaning is what propels them to do the work.

Impact of Work

Do we believe that our work matters to others?

More than ever, the next generation of workers wants to know: "Are we just lining the pockets of the people at the top, or are we making some sort of difference in the world around us?"

Impact of Work asks:

- Do I matter, and does my personal work make an impact?
- Can we win as a team, and does our team have an impact on the results of the organization?
- Are we recognized as a team for the impact that we are making?

If people feel that they personally don't matter and their work is not making a difference, then they are hard-pressed to want to stay in a job and give it their all. They need to know that they matter and that someone cares.

Psychological Safety

Can we take risks and put our ideas out there free of insecurity or embarrassment?

Unsafe teams rarely thrive. They are toxic in all their ways. When you feel safe on a team, that breeds the ability to try new things, take risks, and innovate.

Psychological Safety asks:

- Can I trust you to have my back, and can ideas be shared freely without having them shot down?
- Can we work well together as a team?
- Do we merge our good ideas into one great idea, or are we always fighting for credit?
- Can you have open and honest communication without fear of retribution?
- If I really tell you what I am feeling—respectfully—will you hear what's on my mind?

These five attributes drive home team success. They are straightforward in their application, and if you focus on them, you will see team morale improve. In fact, the success and growth of your organization depend on them.

TAKE ACTION:

- Of the five principles that determine team success, what is your most effective area and your least effective one?
- What can you do to share your most effective area with other teams, so they can glean from you?
- What's your plan to improve your least effective area?

FRAMEWORK TOOLS:

- Idea Socialization Framework

Chapter 3

DOES YOUR CULTURE KILL OR CULTIVATE INNOVATION?

"We can't solve problems by using the same kind of thinking we used when we created them."

—ALBERT EINSTEIN[12]

When consulting with teams, I have them think about their own structure and where they can really have the biggest impact. There are several key areas we dive into explicitly:

- Alignment: Alignment is your secret weapon. (Internal)
- Team Health: Healthy Team, Healthy Results (Internal)
- Empathy vs. Lack of Empathy (External)

12 David Mielach, "We Can't Solve Problems by Using the Same Kind of Thinking We Used When We Created Them," *Business Insider*, 19 Apr. 2012, https://www.businessinsider.com/we-cant-solve-problems-by-using-the-same-kind-of-thinking-we-used-when-we-created-them-2012-4.

ALIGNMENT IS YOUR SECRET WEAPON (GROWING INTERNAL TEAMS)

Have you ever noticed people like to walk down the path of least resistance? Who can blame them for doing so? Where there's no clear plan in place, we tend to experience unnecessary failure in the area of strategic plans. Teams must coordinate and overlay their strategic plans, locate gaps, and adapt to the shifting economic climate if they want to experience real success. If working on ideas together is hard, people will work alone. If getting ideas through the organization is hard, people will launch their own thing on the side. This lack of engagement at work doesn't mean you have bad employees; it means that you haven't earned the right to lead them.

Alignment creates clarity across the organization. It tells everyone this is what matters, and this is what you should be working on. When we see organizations have twenty strategic targets, we see confusion and a lack of focus from the team.

Create between one and five strategic targets, and focus your team or organization on those targets for the year. Talk about them, measure them, and celebrate them.

Create Your Strategic Targets

Your strategic targets are aligned to your vision and mission. Some targets may span years, but the main idea is to break them down and help people think about just a few in the year ahead. Some examples of this might be:

- Enter the European market through organic business launch or through acquisition.

- Create an internal data lake with external implications to create products for customer dashboarding.
- Launch a new product line that serves a new market.

Talk About Your Strategic Targets

Once you've selected your strategic targets, you want to talk about them weekly with your leadership team. Ensure that there's clarity and alignment not just around what you are going to do but how you are going to do it. Not only should these be scoped out by the team, but they also should be treated like a full-blown program or project. There should be milestones, owners, and consistent updates.

Based on Example 1: Enter the European market through organic business launch or through acquisition.

- Engineering: Software development, translation, and localization implications.
- Accounting and Finance: Cost of acquisition, cost to run the business, tax and accounting implications.
- Product Development: How will we merge platforms and over what time frame?

Measure Your Strategic Targets

You've heard the saying that what gets measured is what matters. So measurement should be a key feature of your meetings.

Based on Example 1, here's a sample scorecard idea:

INITIATIVES SCORECARD		MEASUREMENTS BY QUARTER				
Initiatives for 2024	**Business Goals**	**Q1**	**Q2**	**Q3**	**Q4**	**Notes**
Initiative 1: Launch Product Silas	Increase Revenue by 20%	5%	11%	17%	23%	Exceeded Goal
Initiative 2: Customer Engage-ment Project	Increase Customer Retention by 30%	17%	22%	29%	29.5%	Missed Goal
Initiative 3: Scale Internal Systems	Automate 15% of Manual Processes	10%	15%	20%	25%	Exceeded Goal

Celebrate Your Strategic Targets

There is a lost art in celebrating with the team. Strategic targets should be rigorous and in addition to the team's current workload. That means if they won, they won big, and we should celebrate that. Go ahead and put that out before the strategic targets ever roll out. Let them know you plan to celebrate them and how.

Consider This: *The leader that creates the most initiatives doesn't get more credit—especially if it's at the cost of the team. Alignment helps us to call our shots and ensure we aim our organization at the right target.*

If everyone in your organization, from the senior leader to the frontline employee, cannot articulate your strategy for the year, then you do not have one—not one that can be executed by all team members.

HEALTHY TEAMS, HEALTHY RESULTS (HOW WE GROW INTERNAL TEAMS)

Have you ever wondered why it's hard to launch new ideas at some companies and why it's easy at others? If trust, speed, agility, and collaboration are not core values of your company, you may find yourself banging your head against the wall.

Strong organizations work in a high-trust environment, creating team health and driving people toward the outcomes they want to hit as a company. Weak organizations lean on creating policies and procedures to control people's movements and actions. Documentation should release the team's potential and act as a road map to create successful outcomes.

Core values like trust, speed, agility, and collaboration give rise to execution and innovation. Teams that are territorial with their time, talent, and funding find it very hard to collaborate with other teams and, therefore, innovate. If you feel like this is the environment you work in, you may have to slow down to speed up. As discussed in the last chapter, building psychological safety and trust at the center of your teams is one of the most important roles you play as a transformational leader.

Constant disagreements and infighting at work drain our energy and put us in a state of fight, flight, or freeze. Here's what I've seen. You can either have dysfunctional teams or innovation, but it's nearly impossible to have both over a long period of time. If you can't get along, you are not ready to grow. Growth only magnifies problems. You can't ignore those problems or make them go away. Facing problems head-on is the only way to deal with them.

Innovation Principle: If you can't get along, you are not ready to grow. Growth only magnifies problems.

I once worked with a team member named Emma who would hold us hostage with a bad attitude and argue with the team like a bull in a china shop. We would debate the best way to solve a problem, and she would talk over everyone. Then, when the team would finally come to agreement on the path forward, if Emma's idea wasn't chosen, we would pay for it over the next few days with a bad attitude. She constantly lashed out at team members, and the team struggled to help her move forward.

After many meetings to provide her with feedback on what it felt like to be on the receiving end of her response, it was clear that she would rather make excuses than grow through this difficult trait. As a team, we were only as strong as Emma would allow us to be. We had to have a hard conversation during which we asked these questions:

- Do you want to be a part of this team?
- Are you willing to work on your communication with the team?
- Can we talk through the difference between offering pushback and pushing someone over?
- Are you willing to work on how you respond if your ideas are not chosen?
- Are you willing to grow in these blind-spot areas?

Ultimately, our culture and values clashed with hers. Our ways of working and hers did not align, and we were sad to see Emma go. While I have had more turnaround stories than "Let's part ways" stories, I was disappointed we couldn't make it work. She was stealing the team's peace, creating unnecessary conflict, and holding the team back by sowing strife. Don't underestimate the impact one person can have on a team. Dysfunction, if not handled, creates a lack of health on the team.

So, if we all know that dysfunction depletes a team, what gives rise to innovation?

In most organizations, ego gets in the way of innovation and collaboration. It prevents us from really moving forward because everyone is jockeying for their own ideas to be accepted versus building on a set of ideas to make it better. It's interesting that the structure for good team dynamics is very similar to what's required to innovate.

Here's what I have found to be true: when you become someone who wants to focus on innovation or transformation, you must die to yourself, your ego, and your ways of working to embrace a broader mandate. We stop asking, *Who am I?* or *What do I want?* and we start asking, *Who are we?* and *What do we want?*

In the year 2000, Russell Crowe starred as Maximus in a movie called *The Gladiator*.[13] There's a scene where he is in an arena with a small army of gladiators facing several chariots that have an unmistakable advantage. In the past, these gladiators would have fought individually, resulting in their death, one by one. Everyone cheers for the chariots. That's how this game is supposed to be played. However, Maximus decides to flip the script. He uses his leadership and ingenuity to rally the rabble into an organized army that survives the odds. There's this part in the movie where he instructs the other gladiators to interlock their shields and move "as one." In a huge upset, Maximus and his men are victorious with less training and fewer resources because they moved as one.

Ultimately, the team that can move as one is always a better bet than a bunch of individuals who are each talented on their own but can't team together. When we combine our efforts and energy and move in the same direction, we are unstoppable because most organizations are made up of individual players—not powerful teams. The team that can move as one wins almost every time. Focusing on how to create healthy teams gives rise to innovation.

---

13 Ridley Scott, dir. *The Gladiator*, 2000; Universal City, CA: Universal Pictures, 2000.

EMPATHY VS. LACK OF EMPATHY (HOW WE LISTEN, LEARN, AND IDEATE)

Over the years, I have seen large software projects fail because someone had a good idea but there was no clarity on three things:

1. Whom is it for?
2. How will it help them solve problems?
3. How can we gain rapid feedback from many to continue to build on the idea?

Crafting your product around generating a set of solutions creates empathy for the user. Empathy, according to the *Merriam-Webster Dictionary*, is "the action of understanding, being aware of, being sensitive to, and vicariously experiencing the feelings, thoughts, and experience of another of either the past or present without having the feelings, thoughts, and experience fully communicated in an objectively explicit manner."[14]

In the product development world, we spend a great deal of time seeking to understand who our customer is and what pain points we can solve for them. We believe that we cannot effectively sell anything if we don't know our audience.

We don't just do this by talking to customers—which is very important. We also do this by observing them. Yes, we observe customers in their natural habitat, going about their day-to-day. The way they use our product in unintended ways is key to what to build next. The way they solve problems matters, and the problems you observe and hear about are what help craft new features and products. We call this an empathy map. We want to ask a ton of open-ended

14 "Empathy," *Merriam-Webster*, https://www.merriam-webster.com/dictionary/empathy.

questions to help gain insight into what customers (buyers and users) are thinking and feeling. Before building anything, this is a great exercise to do.

When working with one client, we learned that she was creating a community-based product for her ideal persona to develop female leaders. We sat down together to map out age range, gender, and job responsibilities. After interviewing a few women that met these criteria, we were able to fill out the empathy map and really create a lens of who her ideal person was.

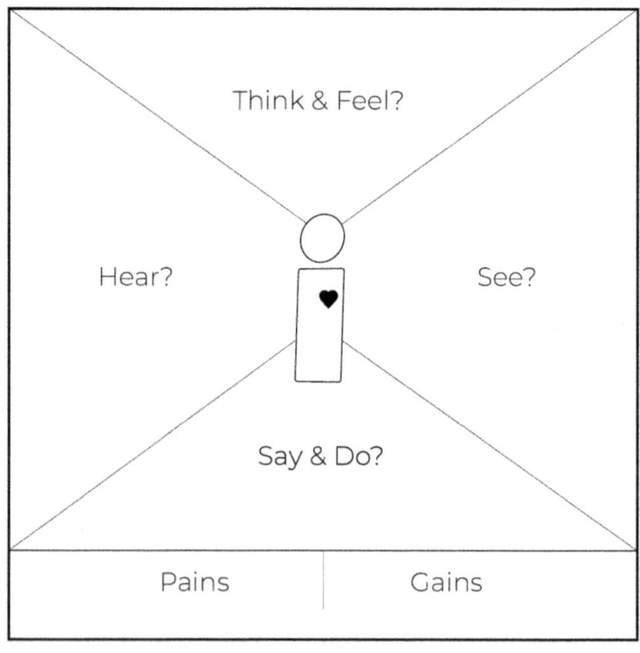

We grouped this into thinking, seeing, saying, doing, hearing, and pains and gains. These areas impact how you can help your ideal customer solve problems. We can't ignore the way our customer thinks or feels simply because it doesn't seem logical to us. Instead, we need to be curious and ask questions.

Consider implementing this method with a female executive in corporate America. All of the following possible questions would be asked of her. And she would provide the possible answers.

Thinking

In order to immerse ourselves in the world of the ideal customer and their industry, we need to read what the customers are reading, follow the same social media accounts, and think like customers are thinking.

Possible questions to ask:

- When it comes to your personal development, what are some of the thoughts you have that you haven't shared with anyone else?
- In the last thirty to ninety days, what are some mindsets you've had about your own personal development?
- Where would personal development fit into your current schedule?
- In the last thirty to ninety days, what are some mindsets you've had about your hobbies?

Possible responses:

- How do I level up my skills?

- How do I keep my business line ahead of what's happening in the market to ensure we have the advantage?
- I know I need to develop myself, but how can I juggle everything that is happening here at work with home, family, and friends?
- Hobbies? What are hobbies?

Seeing

When it comes to the industry you are serving, it is important to understand what your customer is seeing both within their organization and within their industry. What they are seeing also shapes what they believe they should be "doing" themselves.

Possible questions to ask:

- What are you seeing in the industry that gets you excited right now?
- What moves are you seeing your competitors and peers making in the industry?
- What do you see your peers doing about their personal growth and development?

Possible responses:

- Our competitors seem to be bringing products to market faster and getting sales traction quicker than we are.
- My competitors seem to develop a bench of leaders faster than my organization can. Typically, we have to hire from them if we want to build a deeper bench.
- My peers have mentors who are showing them the ropes in business.

Saying

It's important to note here how hard it is to see someone saying one thing but, perhaps, doing another. This is pretty normal customer behavior and, of course, human behavior too. So as you lean into this area, if you feel cognitive dissonance between what they are saying and doing, that is completely normal. In fact, if you can close the gap between the two, you may have a product idea.

Possible questions to ask:

- In the last thirty to ninety days, if your friends asked you what you are doing to develop yourself, what would you say?
- What would need to be true for you to be a part of a development program?
- What would need to be true for you to be part of an executive-level community-based program?

Possible responses:

- I don't have a ton of extra time, and I consume a lot of information on the go.
- It would need to be high value and drive to the point quickly. I would want to be around people in a role similar to the role I am currently in.
- It would have to add a ton of value for me to consider it. I want to network but don't have time for it.

Doing

Observation is a powerful part of this process. During the observation process, we are either asking them to complete certain tasks while we watch or go about their normal day. We are simultaneously looking for areas of opportunity.

Possible questions to ask:

- Where do you go for development?
- What skill-building areas have you looked up in the last thirty to ninety days?

Possible responses:

- I peruse periodicals like the Harvard Business Review, The Economist, and other news sources.
- I read articles or watch videos about negotiating for a higher salary in alignment with my role, organizing and running large teams, and closing large and complex deals.

You may also observe the following:

- She is using her phone to consume content regularly.
- She is in back-to-back meetings, busy, and with not a lot of time on her hands.
- She is multitasking when she's watching a developmental video—trying to eat lunch and respond to a text.

Hearing

What is your client hearing? We want to know what is influencing them. These may be things they are hearing at their office, from their friends, etc.

Possible questions to ask:

- What are some of the trends you are hearing in your industry about women in leadership and the intersection of development?

- What are some things you are hearing from your office about women in leadership and the intersection of development?

Possible responses:

- We are still not doing enough to prepare women for higher-level leadership roles.
- Women often feel flat-footed when being tapped for stretch roles in our organization.

Feeling

What is your client thinking and feeling? What does your client worry about, and what preoccupies their thoughts?

Possible questions to ask:

- How do you feel about your overall job responsibilities?
- How do you feel you're doing when it comes to your personal development?
- How are those in your reporting structure feeling?

Possible responses:

- I feel pressure from my leaders and shareholders to produce more with less.
- I feel overwhelmed when it comes to finding the time for personal development.
- I love my work but must balance the feelings of constant pressure to perform, burnout, and exhaustion due to my workload.

Pains

What are their pains? Help your client surface fears, frustrations, and obstacles. The sooner you do this, the sooner you can find unique ways to solve them.

Possible questions to ask:

- Tell me about your top three pain points in the last ninety days with your development or personal leadership.

Possible responses:

- I am overwhelmed with not enough hours for personal development.
- I'm feeling the pressure to level up specific executive-level skills.
- There is not enough time in the day to spend on personal development.

Our goal is to take all of the feedback regarding these pain points and ask the question: *How can we solve some of the key challenges?*

Gains

What are your client's gains? Now it's time to figure out their wants, needs, and how they are measuring success.

Possible questions to ask:

- When it comes to your personal development, when was the last time you felt successful?
- Why did you feel you were winning?
- What led to that?

Possible responses:

- I feel successful whenever I have the tools, skills, and resources to effectively do my job.
- When I furthered my career, I felt like I was winning.
- Having access to a network of like-minded leaders who provided feedback made it easier to identify my wins.

Out of that empathy map, you may ideate on a few concepts like:

- Curated development daily based on her career goals delivered to her phone.
- Creating a community and network she has access to 24/7.
- Gamification to help her remain engaged one to two times per day.

It's important to be able to speak to your client's needs and concerns.

FOUR WAYS TO LISTEN

1. **Coffee Conversations**—If you are not sure, take your ideal customer or client to coffee and ask.
2. **Listening Sessions**—Set up intentional time to interview multiple potential customers at the same time.
3. **Surveys**—Deploy a survey to your ideal customer base, and ask some key questions.
4. **Observation**—Listening with our eyes is just as important as listening with our ears, so ask to observe your ideal customers for a bit and take notes.

What questions are you afraid to ask your customers? They might be painful to hear, but they could also unlock something new. When times are uncertain, we must disrupt our norms. Our norm is usually to hide instead of advance, especially when people start talking about economic issues and recessions. Once you've built your empathy map, you have what you need to begin to build out a persona or multiple personas for your product.

BUILDING OUT YOUR PERSONAS

When working with the American female executive, we created her ideal persona. She had two profiles that were important to her: the rising leader and the established leader. Let's look at an example of the rising leader.

"The Rising Leader" Persona

- **Name**—It's important to name your persona so that you can refer to it.
- **Picture**—Select a picture of a real person. I prefer real over a sketch or a cartoon so that you can empathize with them.
- **Personality Type**—Think about their personality type. It is helpful to even have a client share their Myers-Briggs or other personality profile.[15]
- **Skills**—What are some of the skills your persona is bringing to the table? Are they tech-savvy, hardworking, or well-organized?
- **Demographics**—Are they married or single? How old are they? Do they have any children? Where do they live? All of these things help us to better connect with our persona.

15 "MBTI Basics," *The Myers & Briggs Foundation - MBTI® Basics*, https://www.myersbriggs.org/my-mbti-personality-type/mbti-basics/.

- **Goals**—What are the goals of the persona? Maybe they want to maximize their time or save time. It's important to know what's driving them to use your product or service.
- **Quote**—I love grabbing a quote from one of your real interviews. This quote becomes an anchor point for how we are going to think about this persona.
- **Background**—Have your client share their career background, how long they have been in their role, and perhaps a few other roles they were in before this one. Understanding their career path and trajectory helps us to relate to them better.
- **Motivations**—What motivates your customer or user? Is it price, convenience, or comfort?
- **Frustrations**—Knowing your customer's core frustrations gives us those future products and services that we will one day build to meet their needs. It also helps us to understand what we should avoid doing.
- **Technology and Platforms**—What technology does your customer use? This could be browsers or even social media platforms.
- **Brands**—What brands does your customer enjoy?

The most important next step is to print out your persona and hang him or her around the office. This important step enables us to act on the golden rule of innovation: put your customer at the center of everything you build. Once you have clarity around what your customer is thinking, and you've nailed your persona, it's time to iterate to arrive at the right set of solutions.

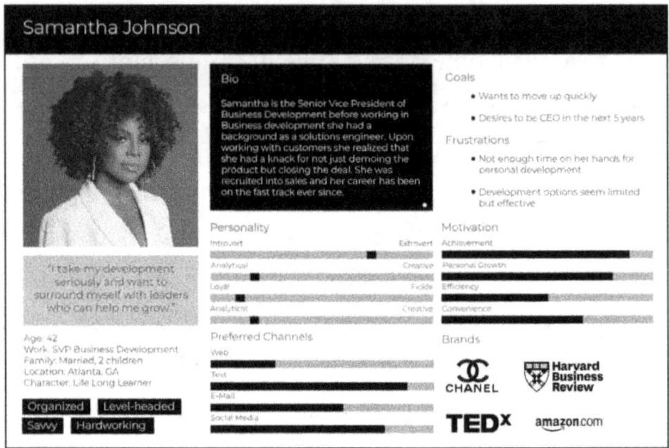

TAKE ACTION:

1. There are three key areas that give rise to innovation:
   - What one area do you need to focus on this year?
   - What's one area you are doing well?
   - How can you replicate that area in other parts of your organization?
2. Do you know your ideal customer or client? What steps can you take today to sit down with three key customers?
3. What did you learn about your customers that you didn't know?
4. How can you apply this new knowledge to your business?

FRAMEWORKS:

- Strategic Objectives
- Empathy Maps
- Personas

Chapter 4

GET OUT THERE AND SEE THE WORLD—THE ULTIMATE SOCIALIZATION FRAMEWORK

"If you look at history, innovation doesn't come just from giving people incentives; it comes from creating environments where their ideas can connect."

—STEVEN JOHNSON[16]

When given the choice, breaking down silos is hard, and opting out is easy. I found that building out a socialization framework helped me stage-gate the idea and get better traction. It became a forcing function, a moment of pause in the product development process to assess, discuss, and realign.

16 "Kevin Kelly and Steven Johnson on Where Ideas Come From," *Wired*, 27 Sept. 2010, https://www.wired.com/2010/09/mf-kellyjohnson/.

As a leader in innovation, this socialization framework will help move your teams from idea to concept and from concept to execution within an organizational setting. This will help teams flesh the idea out before pitching it. Start with discovery by building an informal or formal team, validate by socializing ideas with the customer, and pitch your fleshed-out idea internally.

INTERNAL DISCOVERY—BUILD THE DREAM TEAM

Innovation is no longer about brilliant individuals; it's about brilliant teams. Whenever we are dreaming up a new product or idea, we want to select a cross-functional team. People from all parts of the organization can speak to this idea. For example, while not an exhaustive list, you may want to include finance, account management, sales, and frontline workers. Why? Because all of these different roles have a pulse on the organization from a different vantage point.

Innovation Principle: Innovation is no longer about brilliant individuals; it's about brilliant teams.

Frontline workers can tell you why customers complain. Account managers can tell you what features clients get excited about and why they renew. The sales team not only knows what customers will buy, but they also know a great deal about the competitive landscape. They know which competitors are eating their lunch. And finance sees all the financial trends in their data. Finance can also help by creating financial projections for your future product based on the success of other products historically.

When you are thinking about who to bring to the table, consider choosing several "zero-gravity" thinkers to take this journey with you. Former Intel innovation strategist Cynthia Barton Rabe says that "zero-gravity thinkers [should not be] weighed down by the expertise of a team, its politics, or the way things have always been done."[17] The more thinking partners and trusted advisors you have in your corner, the better.

Zero-gravity thinkers will not hold back how they feel or what they think of your solution. These honest opinions will allow your team to reach an optimal outcome at a faster rate. It feels good to have people agree with our ideas, but reassurance doesn't always allow for progress. Zero-gravity thinkers will challenge the status quo and create new thoughts and ideas that push us outside of our comfort zones.

When it comes to discovering what we can build and how we can build it, we need to avoid surrounding ourselves with "yes" people and start surrounding ourselves with people who question: *What if? How can we?* and *Why?*

EXTERNAL VALIDATION—ITERATE OR DIE—THERE IS NO PERFECT

Innovation Principle: If you are holding an idea until it is perfect, you've probably missed your moment.

17 Cynthia Barton Rabe, *Innovation Killer: How What We Know Limits What We Can Imagine and What Smart Companies Are Doing About It* (New York, NY: AMACOM, 2022).

Over the years, through economic downturns and pandemics, we have learned that business moves at the speed of light. Those who didn't respond quickly to change went out of business.

You see, iterating is the simple act of acknowledging that whatever we do will not be perfect out of the gate. It also helps us to understand that if we are waiting for perfection, we will never release value to those that are waiting for it. Instead of trying to get it perfect, let processes, products, or whatever you are launching grow alongside the people for whom you are launching it.

When we hold back ideas because of perfectionism, we stifle creativity. But when we invite others to interact with our ideas, something powerful happens. The idea gets even better than it would have been had we hoarded it and kept it all to ourselves.

This type of iteration is so much easier with healthy teams. *Merriam-Webster* defines iterating as doing something again and again.[18] It allows us to rapidly take in feedback without being hurt by others' opinions but instead allowing that information to make us better.

Do we see the feedback we receive from those we serve as a gift? If a customer or an employee is bold enough to tell you something is not working, have the courage to listen, and then rapidly grow and develop that idea further based on that feedback. Most of us are in the business of solving problems for others, so iterating helps us solve their problems more rapidly. Perfectionism steals the seeds you should sow today by telling you it would be better to sow them

---

18 "Iterate Definition & Meaning," *Merriam-Webster*, https://www.merriam-webster.com/dictionary/iterate.

tomorrow. Kick perfectionism to the curb in service of those that you serve every day.

The Napkin Sketch

Once your idea is sketched out on a napkin or a simple piece of paper, it's time to get into the field and start talking to customers about the idea. The number one concern I see in organizations is that they wait too long to reach this step. Start EARLY!

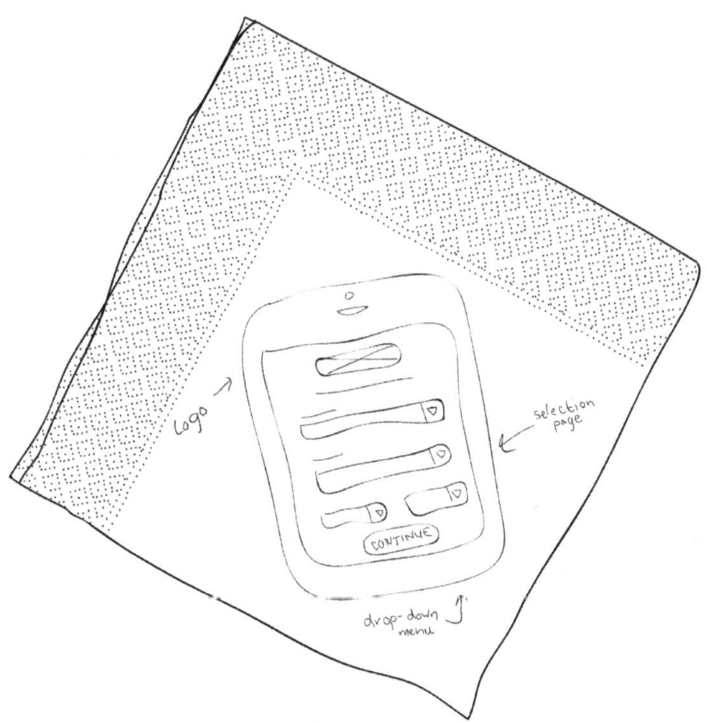

What You Need to Get into the Field

1. **The Idea**—Start socializing the idea to learn if people are really interested.
2. **Value Proposition**—This is your elevator pitch. In an elevator, you have less than a minute until the door opens. If you can't say it quickly and succinctly, you have more work to do.
3. **Benefits**—What are the benefits to the customer when they use this product? There should be between three and five clear benefits.
4. **Napkin Sketch**—Don't build anything high-resolution until you have low-resolution agreement that the idea works.
5. **Ballpark Pricing**—When in front of the customer, don't hesitate to find their price sensitivity. Learn how much they are willing to pay for the product.

Example Product Idea

1. **Product Idea**—A Faster Way to Do Taxes
2. **Value Proposition**—We believe taxes are not a one-time event. We've set up machine learning and AI to help ensure your taxes are done in real time, and you can estimate the amount you will pay in taxes down to $100. No big surprises. Know what you owe!
3. **Benefits**—
    - Know where you stand well before April 15.
    - Access a real-time snapshot, so there are no surprises.
    - Receive projections and suggestions to put you in the best possible tax position.

4. **Low-Resolution Sketches**—Show between five and ten low-resolution sketches to help potential clients understand how the user interface will function without going all in.
5. **Ballpark Price**—Show the ballpark price for this product as a subscription model. Can you take a look at these price ranges and tell us how much you would pay annually based on the value you would receive? (We think people will always select the lower price, but that's not necessarily accurate. Often, customers want the right value for the right price.)
   - $10-$25 a month/per seat | $120-$300 annually
   - $26-$55 a month/per seat | $312-$660 annually
   - $56-$80 a month/per seat | $672-$960 annually

This process is designed to help you receive answers in days—not months. If the idea, value proposition, benefits, and low-resolution sketches are not resonating, it's time to go back to the drawing board. There's more work to be done.

Consider This: *Take three to five value propositions to the customer meeting and see if there's one that really resonates with them. Often people don't want to shoot down your "one idea," but if you come with a few different ideas, you will see movement around discussion of what resonates and what does not.*

BUYERS AND USERS

In the last chapter, through engaging with buyers and users, we built alignment around their needs, built personas, and began to generate new ideas to help them solve key problems. Now we need to decide exactly where the focus should be directed and understand why your solution is or isn't working. This research is a critical part of knowing if you have interest and buy-in before you go all in.

When we talk to the right people early, we avoid investing in something that may not have legs in the market or fall within our sphere of influence. The principle of failing fast makes sense when the proper work has been done. However, most ideas fail because necessary guardrails haven't been put up to stop innovations early when we see that there's no appetite for what we are building.

Innovation Principle: Feedback gives innovators guardrails to see the early signs of success or failure.

Feedback helps innovators understand where the needs are and allows for laser-like focus in their approach versus those who throw spaghetti at the wall and see what sticks. When handled correctly, this framework creates the building blocks for success and early indicators of failure.

Armed with research, it's time to pitch the idea by using a series of sketches. We will use this to interact with potential users and buyers.

In this process, it is best to hold ideas loosely.

Sample Script

Here's a sample script to talk to customers:

Thank you, Kim, for allowing us to come pick your brain for about thirty minutes on this new product idea. We are counting on your absolute honesty. We expect to hear things like "I don't like that," or "It would work better if." Don't pull any punches. You are the client we are aiming to reach, so if this doesn't work for you, or you wouldn't buy it, we need to know that now!

First, let's cover the value proposition and benefits. Upon hearing that, what thoughts come to mind? What pushback do you have? What did and did not work well?

(Note: I am not asking, how much do you like my pitch? I am asking questions that invite the customer to push back now as opposed to when I have something built.)

Next, I'd like you to take a look at this series of sketches. Together, we are going to talk through how these would work and where you might have questions. What would you change? Where was it confusing? What resonated with you?

Our final question is this: Would you buy a product like this with the modifications you mentioned?

Please look at these sample prices. What would you be willing to pay monthly or annually for a product like this?

Thank you for your time!

Note: As a bonus, provide your client with some type of free product or gift card. Your simple appreciation will go a long way.

You can do this type of product or idea rationalization as a group or one-on-one. Doing this as a group is faster; however, be careful of groupthink. We are looking for important patterns that will help us make good decisions, and often, when people get together, they can tend to take on the opinions of the crowd even if their thoughts may differ. This is where asking several follow-up questions will help to get to the bottom of people's actual thoughts.

BATCHING FEEDBACK

As you receive feedback from your customers, you can group that feedback into a few key buckets:

- **Out of Scope**—Some features and solutions requested will be out of scope for the phase of the product you are working on. Some will be out of scope completely as in something that is not on your radar to build or provide.
- **Small Changes**—Small changes are classified as moving a button or changing a workflow, so it's less confusing. Small changes can then be batched and prioritized.
- **Large Changes**—Large changes might include a fundamental rewrite of your database, user flow, or key layouts. While these changes can feel huge, if you receive a pattern that something needs to change, you have to plan for it. Break it down into smaller projects and begin the evolution of the product.
- **Product Backlog**—Your product backlog will consist of good suggested changes that you can work on now or later. That backlog will require prioritization so that everyone knows which changes are most important.

PITCHING THE IDEA INTERNALLY

After your customer session, you will make necessary tweaks to your design. You can do one more round of feedback, and then endeavor to make the idea official. Either way, don't let the pitch phase fool you; you are not out of the woods yet. You will take the feedback you receive and begin to iterate through it in order to learn.

When we come out of the pitch phase, we don't hold our idea precious; we expect a few more rounds of discovery, validation, and pitching before we can really confirm that the idea is real. Iteration happens rapidly, so don't be alarmed. When iteration is done right, it allows us to always be learning, growing, and expanding the way we solve problems and deliver solutions.

What might your pitch look like?

1. Validated Value Proposition
2. Validated Benefits
3. Updated Sketches and Pricing
4. Key Quotes and Financial Commitments from Customers
5. Financial Projects for the Product (3-, 6-, 12-month growth)
6. Timeline to Build the Feature

Keep it simple, and learn from every point of feedback. Use that feedback to make the idea stronger.

Why do most organizations find this type of collaboration extremely hard? Often, it's because the organization has not focused on documenting its systems and processes. When organizational maturity is low, innovation feels impossible because most organizations are just reacting to chaos. When the organization can wrap its mind around creating systems and processes, innovation can more sustainably be built on top of a firm foundation. If your foundation is weak, your innovations will not see the light of day. So let's talk about maturity models and how they help innovation.

TAKE ACTION:

1. What can you do to release ideas faster as opposed to holding onto them?
2. Knowing your value proposition is powerful. Many organizations just don't know how to quickly, succinctly, and fluently say what they provide and why it matters. What about you? Does your organization do this well? At all levels? Plan a half day as a team to focus on creating or refining your value proposition. Then practice pitching to one another for further refinement.
3. What's one idea your team has been kicking around for a while now? How can you go from idea to product faster? Use the format above to generate some rapid feedback from your customers.

FRAMEWORKS:

- Napkin Sketch
- The Socialization Framework

Chapter 5
IT'S TIME TO GROW UP

"Weak systems make great people look bad. Strong systems make good people look great."

—CRAIG GROESCHEL[19]

I once worked in an organization where the leader would ask, "Why are we not more innovative?" but when you looked at three things in the organization—pace, process, and empowerment—I thought the answer was pretty obvious.

Have you ever seen Lucille Ball in the "At the Chocolate Factory" clip?[20] It shows perfectly the way that organization was run. In that scene, they put Lucy and Ethel on an assembly line to wrap chocolates. The conveyor belt was moving so fast that Lucy and Ethel had

19 Mike Vierow, "4 Areas to Focus Your Leadership, Part 2: Life.church Open Network," *Life. Church Open Network Blog*, 8 Mar. 2018, https://openblog.life.church/4-areas-to-focus-your-leadership-part-2/.
20 "I Love Lucy | Lucy and Ethel at the Chocolate Factory (S2, E1) | Paramount+," *YouTube*, 30 Aug. 2022, https://www.youtube.com/watch?v=AnHiAWIrYQc.

to improvise to keep up. The supervisor came back and saw that they were doing "okay" without really checking on them or the quality of their work. (Both women had chocolates hidden in their pockets, mouths, hats, and blouses.) They were actually in real trouble.

The supervisor, however, yelled out, "Speed it up a little!" which threw the two of them into all-out chaos. The most heartbreaking statement of this whole scene was when Lucy said, "Ethel, I think we are fighting a losing game." Lucy and Ethel were grabbing chocolates, filling their hats, and throwing chocolate down their blouses, and while comically it's hilarious, it, unfortunately, is a perfect example of the three areas in which most organizations fail their people:

1. Pace
2. Process
3. Empowerment

These three capacities will make or break an organization.

THE PACE

If your pace is too slow, not only do you lull the organization to sleep, but your competition will also eat your lunch. If the pace is too fast, it becomes sink or swim for everyone who comes into your organization. It's dog-eat-dog, and not many will survive. If they make it through onboarding and manage to hang on for dear life, they will end up burned out later.

Innovation Principle: Pace matters.

People often believe that all of their employees must be booked at 90 percent or even 120 percent of their capacity. When we do that, we are not leaving room for emergencies, fires, and—even more important—creativity and innovation. When we run our teams at 90 percent capacity or higher, we also lead them into burnout, causing them to become less productive.

It's in the downtime that our brains have an opportunity to recover. The downtime enables us to think innovatively. At this particular organization, people would say, "I feel like I have to constantly check my phone," and "I don't know the priority of anything, so I feel like I have to treat everything as urgent." Even worse, "I don't know how I can vacation or rest because I always feel like I am behind." When you begin to hear this type of sentiment in teams, I can assure you they are already burned out or quickly barreling toward it.

If your organization lacks pace and rhythm, surprise meetings, surprise projects, and tons of emergencies constantly pop up. But we are not making plans for people's vacations, learning, and rest.

Free your team to operate at 60-80 percent capacity when working to execute on projects because with interruptions, this is a more accurate assessment of their bandwidth. Isolate an eight-hour day. That means they have between 4.8 and 6.4 hours to work on project execution. The rest of their time is spent in meetings, breaks, and various interruptions that take place throughout the day.

This will open room for thinking, tinkering, and dreaming. Creativity doesn't often come through stress and being under the gun. It might, perhaps, for some, but for most, it comes from having the capacity and bandwidth to dream.

LACK OF PROCESSES

Often, teams do not have formalized processes documented, and as a result, they have to recreate the wheel every time they need to begin a significant project. They don't have clear stakeholder matrices, so people are not sure whom to include on projects, and more often than not, important stakeholders are left off of the project.

Having a project framework that everyone can point to, use, and follow is part of an organization's maturity. When this is absent, it takes longer to work with the right teams and even figure out whom we are supposed to work with or how to engage them.

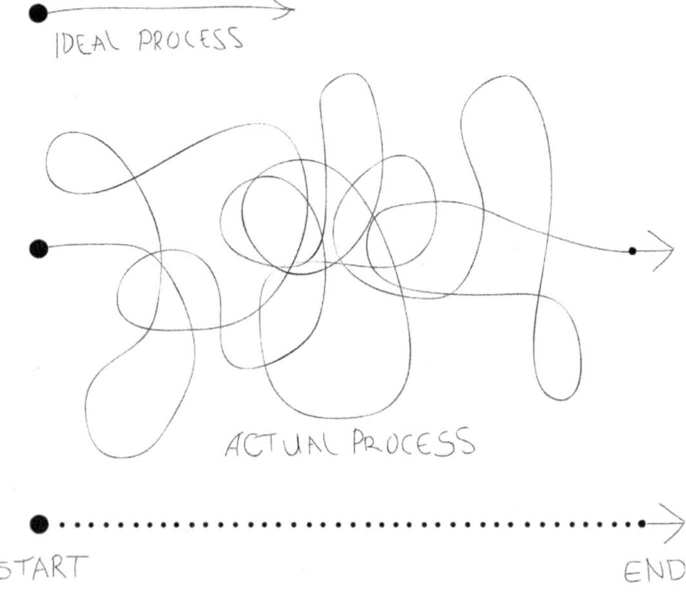

These types of projects typically deliver over budget and below expectations. There's no improving the process or even providing status as to where the project is. A lack of systems and processes prevents product and service delivery. Having formalized processes in an organization helps everyone understand where and how to get things done. More on this later in the chapter.

EMPOWERMENT

The third challenge is that those at the top are the only ones allowed to have brilliant ideas. How do we know this lack of empowerment is happening? Most things are rolled out without talking to frontline employees. Most people are not asked for their opinions. There is no formal way to intake good ideas, and if someone has a good idea, it must be passed up the chain of command. They are not allowed to run with it. Typically, one or a few people get all the credit for all the hard work that everyone else has done.

If you want to empower, you must find ways to do four core things:

1. Ask the frontliners for their observations, opinions, and advice.
2. Find formal and informal ways to cultivate their ideas.
3. When a good idea emerges, allow them to run with the idea, and give them the credit and support they need to see it through.
4. Allow them to fail in a safe environment, so they can learn.

So, how mature is your organization when it comes to these three areas: pace, processes, and empowerment? These areas help or hurt an organization's ability to innovate. The Capability Maturity Model

Integration (CMMI) starts by helping us understand where we are in relation to an intended practice area.

CMMI MATURITY MODEL

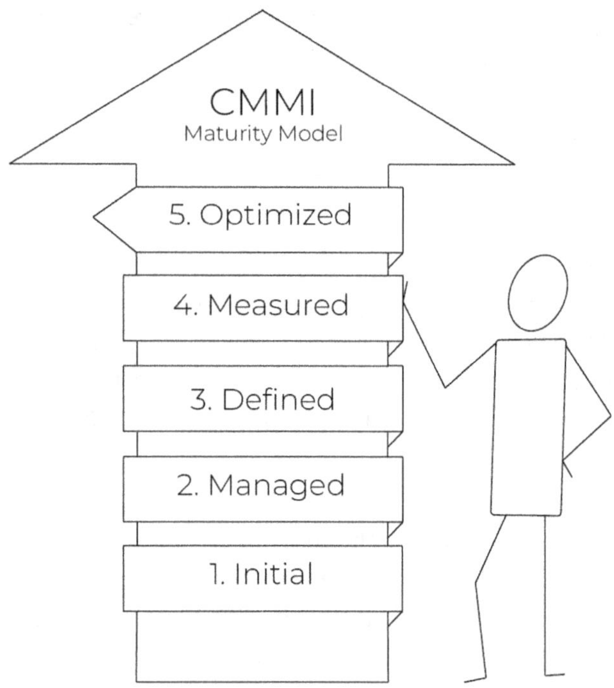

Several years ago, I worked with an organization to bring their capability maturity up in the area of project management. They wanted to raise the capabilities of the organization across the board. They felt like most of their functions—IT, project management, and business analysis—were failing. Their customers on the marketing side were complaining and unsatisfied with the service they were receiving.

Instead of getting angry, this leader decided to roll up his sleeves and figure out how to fix most of the key issues. It all started with customer interviews, employee interviews, and a better understanding of what systems and processes were already in place. They had inconsistencies across the board and hovered around a level 0 for most functions in their organization.

The maturity index goes from level 0 (the lowest) to level 5 (the highest). Most organizations can reach level 3 and are fairly pleased with their results. Getting from one level to the next can take anywhere from twelve to eighteen months if you really focus on it. The organization I worked with was a large multinational, and they knew they were signing up for about a four- to five-year transformation plan.

Step one was to pull up all the rocks and look at the squiggly things that were underneath. It was not pretty. They surveyed customers and users, and it was like exposing all the bad things that had been hidden in the closets for years. The people who were helping to hide those things so as not to improve them were asked to find opportunities elsewhere. Road maps were created with accountability to move the organization from level 0 to level 3, with milestones and stage-gates along the way. A four-year vision to get from here to there was born. But it all began with asking questions.

Do you have a product development process or life cycle?

A product development life cycle depicts how you can go from:

- Idea and Concept

- Understanding the feasibility
- Design and Development
- Production and Deployment
- Continuous Improvement
- Sunsetting or Phasing out the product

How do you measure innovation success?

Measuring success looks like understanding what quantitative and qualitative data you are looking for before you begin. Things like ROI, revenue, sales, user adoption, etc.

Level 0—Inconsistent

The challenge with being at level 0 is that there are few to no disciplines or controls in place for your organization in any area that you manage. That means innovation may or may not be happening. It also means everyone does things differently. When there's no playbook, process, or procedure that aligns a team's behaviors, there's no ability to scale. In fact, lack of organizational discipline means you're planning to NOT innovate.

Innovation Principle: Lack of organizational discipline means you're planning to NOT innovate.

At level 0, if you have ten people doing the same role, it means they all do the same task ten different ways. It also means most information is tribal knowledge; it exists in people's heads but is not documented anywhere. Tribal knowledge is passed down verbally from one person to the next. It also implies that if the person leaves, they take that knowledge with them. When it comes to developing products, a process enables us to create a way for all ideas to be surfaced, good ideas to be tested, and the best ideas to be launched into the market.

Level 1—Initial

At level 1, work can be unpredictable and reactive but only addresses performance issues within the process. Work is completed but can often be over budget or delayed. This is still a challenging environment to innovate in because there are very few real controls in place. Think of it as a chaotic environment. Level 1 projects are typically completed as a result of heroic effort on the part of the teams—not because we have the right controls in place. Teams are delivering work in spite of the lack of processes and controls.

Level 2—Managed

When you move to level 2, the focus is on creating managed projects. So when projects are initiated, there are controls around said projects but not necessarily organizational controls in place. Projects are planned, performed, measured, monitored, and controlled. The focus is on project performance.

In level 2 maturity, we begin to adhere to plans such as documented organizational plans, processes, and policies. We designate the right funding, tools, and people for critical projects. We also have a clear understanding of the stakeholder matrix, and we are ensuring that we use that stakeholder matrix for communication and proper dissemination of information. As it concerns projects, we also review the process and its work products and address anything that doesn't align or comply. In this phase, most of what we are focused on applies to projects but not necessarily having organizational controls.

Level 3—Defined

As organizations move from level 2 to level 3, there's a foundation in place that enables the company to leverage organizational standards. These standards allow projects to use organizational assets that did not exist in level 2. The key here is that at level 3, actions begin to be proactive—not reactive. Organizational-wide standards are in place that provides guidance for projects, programs, and portfolios.

The big difference between level 2 and 3 is that at level 2, these processes are confined to projects. At level 3, they are now applied organizationally. That means processes are performed consistently across the organization. If you think about it, being at least level 3 ensures that we don't get into what we discussed earlier: creating the same product in three different countries. Now, we can leverage economies of scale to help the organization build out our product, leveraging processes one time across the organization. This also means we can learn from other projects' success and fail points. That's a big deal.

Level 4—Quantitatively Measured

Most organizations don't make it past level 3 because it gets harder and more expensive to manage. The organization is data-driven with clear quantitative performance measurements in place. Objectives are predictable and aligned to ensure they meet the goals of internal and external stakeholders.

Level 5—Optimized

When organizations focus on continuous improvement, they've now reached level 5 organization. They are built to pivot and respond to the changing landscape, and at this level, they can really provide a platform for true agility. They can control their projects with real-time data. These organizations are seen as stable and flexible. This is a breeding ground for innovation.

Innovation Principle: Words like discipline and process are not stiflers to innovation.

Many people think that discipline and documentation stifle innovation, but when we don't have discipline, we are planning NOT to innovate. Words like discipline and process are not stiflers to innovation. They, instead, tell us where to focus and how to focus. Discipline and process in the organization help us uncover our true north, unlocking innovation. When we don't have to recreate the wheel every time we start or end a project, we free up mental space for innovation. And things that we do constantly we can document and operationalize, so everyone else knows how those processes run.

We, on purpose, kill this idea of tribal knowledge where you must find the tribe leader to even understand what is happening. Now, you democratize information so that anyone and everyone can find out how to run a certain set of processes. When the tribe leader leaves, it doesn't hurt the people that remain because they understand where the information is and how to leverage it to continue success.

At levels 0-2, we call a shot, hope we hit it, and may or may not have any way to measure its success. At levels 3-5 we call our shots, and the processes exist for the organization to support our shot and to measure it. Chaos doesn't breed innovation, but good systems and processes support the innovation that you want to build.

LEADING FOR CHANGE

Now, let's be honest. Everything I just covered requires a change: in mindset, ways of working, and systems and processes. I can remember distinctly being asked to take on such a change project years ago. I was between a rock and a hard place. While I had a job I absolutely loved, I was asked to consider a new opportunity within the organization. As I sat across from the CIO, he warned me it would be like taking on a turnaround and a startup at the same time. He said if I was up for the challenge, I would have the chance to build something great from the ground up. What he didn't tell me was that the teams involved were jaded, cynical, and seemingly unmovable. I was unaware of the mountain that lay ahead of me.

Leading Change Is Brutal

In my new role, I had a dotted line of over one hundred practitioners reporting to me. I decided it would be best to start with focus groups; I wanted to learn more about everyone's experiences from the ground up. In the first of many roundtables, I sat down with six people. It became immediately clear that one woman—let's call her Cassandra—was the most vocal. As the roundtable progressed, tensions started to rise. I continued to ask for the whole truth and nothing but the truth. Cassandra was more than happy to oblige.

She leaned in with confidence and said, "There have been three changes of the guard since I've been here. There's no point in changing. I am not sure how long you will be here, but I am going to outlast you, just like I've outlasted every other leader who has been in this role."

Immediately, I understood that if I didn't win over Cassandra and her followers, I would not be able to bring about the change I wanted to see for this organization. Since the box was already wide open, I asked her my final question: "Is there anything else you'd like me to know?"

She responded, "Yes. What gives you the right to lead us? I looked at your background, and you don't have the certifications that we have. Technically, I am more qualified than you to do this job."

That was the perfect question for her to ask. I leaned in and stated, "Cassandra, this job was available for anyone to apply. If you felt you could have done it better, I wish you would have applied. That being said, I am happy to get any certification you think would help me better understand your role and responsibilities. At the moment, I am in this role because the status quo is no longer working. I am in this role because we must effect change together. My main goals are these: I want this department to win and gain back the credibility that it's lost over the years. I know my words alone will not convince you, but I hope you will also take note of my actions."

I asked if she would be willing to be part of the committee I was forming to effect change. I noted that her tenure could be helpful to us since she had already seen what was not effective and what did not work. She agreed to help. It was a small win and a step in the right direction.

Leading Change Takes Credibility

It is well-known that the fastest way for a leader to lose credibility is to say one thing and do another. Ignoring problems and failing to act when action is required could lead to further disaster. While most leaders naturally want to surround themselves with people who agree with them and never challenge their leadership, I knew I would never effect change that way. If I had walked away from that conversation with Cassandra and decided to ignore and avoid her (as I may have wanted to do), I would have been a figurehead in a role with no real power to make a difference.

Every organization contains people who hold a certain power base (political support or influence), and Cassandra had that power base on lockdown. To accomplish anything, I would have to go straight to the source of power. It was not my superior who held all the power. It was my subordinate. However, you can't lead based on position or title. You have to earn the right to lead others. This is a tough pill to swallow because it requires you to roll up your sleeves and join the fight with them, shoulder to shoulder and toe to toe. Within six months, I had obtained every certification Cassandra had. I wasn't going to allow a piece of paper to prevent me from having credibility with the team. I still had to find a way to transform the way people saw our organization, but this was just the start.

Leading Change Requires Accountability

I created several teams made up of the most vocal, frustrated people, and each time we met, we dove straight into the heart of the matter. Leading change can't just be about allowing people to air their grievances. I challenged them to provide me with real solutions to the specific problems they raised. We whiteboarded those solutions, and I sent them out to test them. If the test was operational, we began to document, educate others on the change, and implement those changes across the board.

As you lead change, hold people accountable to become part of the solution rather than exclusively presenting all the problems. Leaders often feel like they have to solve these problems alone, but sometimes, the best person to solve the problem is the one who sees it. I continued to tell the team: "If you are gifted to see the problem, you are gifted to solve it."

Leading Change Requires Vision

As meetings with team members continued, we quickly realized that this change journey was bigger than us. We needed to put together a visual image that would tell the story. This resulted in a one-page visual description to talk about the change with our stakeholders. This one-page vision depicted the team's feedback and the acknowledgment that both operations and morale weren't where they should be. In the image, we created a bridge from where we were to where we wanted to go. Under the bridge, we showed all the processes and practices we were going to implement to get us from point A to B. This vision did several things for us:

- It made our stakeholders feel heard while providing them with a vision of what the future looked like with their partnership.
- It gave internal teams clarity on our true north as it eliminated confusion about where we were going and the tactics used to get there.

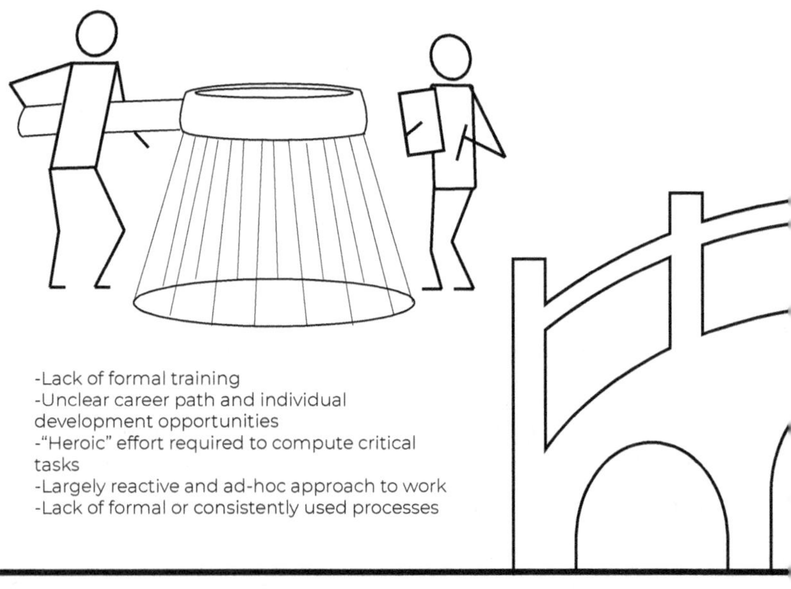

- It helped us decide what to say "yes" versus "no" to. When new initiatives came in, we used this vision to determine whether or not we should work on or invest in the ideas.
- It helped our leaders understand and buy into the transformational journey we were on.

Our Ambition

-Internal formalized training
-Clear career paths and development opportunities
-Shared best practices and lessons learned
-Established processes
-More predictable delivery and alignment
-Lower cost of doing business and achieving organizational goals

trategy Enabler

Support & Consideration

Visuals not only transmit messages to the brain more quickly, but they also help people make decisions faster. Remember, this principle is not only powerful; it has longevity, and we see this verse in the book of Habakkuk 2:2 (ESV): "Write the vision; make it plain on tablets, so he may run who reads it."

When you write a vision down and create visual imagery around it, you are democratizing that vision so that others can run with it. You take it out of your head and put it in their hands. This is one of the most important and impactful facets of leading change. The people you lead must see, know, and understand the vision. If they don't, that vision is dead on arrival.

Write it down, share it visually, and make it clear. A leader's job is to continually keep the vision in front of the people. It's true that when you grow tired of hearing yourself repeat the vision, others are finally starting to understand it. Studies show people must hear something between seven and ten times before it starts to sink in.[21] Stating the vision once is the first step of many.

Leading Change Is Emotional

When looking at the Kübler-Ross Change Curve, it's easy to recognize that change is emotional.[22] Shock and surprise are the immediate reactions, quickly followed by denial. When I first sat down with Cassandra, she was stuck between shock and denial and barreling toward frustration. But the morale journey doesn't stop

---

21 "What Is the Rule of 7? (plus Why It's Important)," *Indeed*, 30 Sept. 2022, https://www.indeed.com/career-advice/career-development/rule-of-seven.

22 Simon Buehring, "Kubler Ross Change Curve," *Knowledge Train*, 29 Jul. 2021, https://www.knowledgetrain.co.uk/change-management/change-management-courses/change-management-models/kubler-ross-change-curve.

there; downright depression can eventually set in as a team undergoes this journey to change. Later, as experimentation begins and the team tries new things, they begin to climb out of that pit of despair. They start seeing themselves as a part of the change versus seeing the change as something that is happening to them.

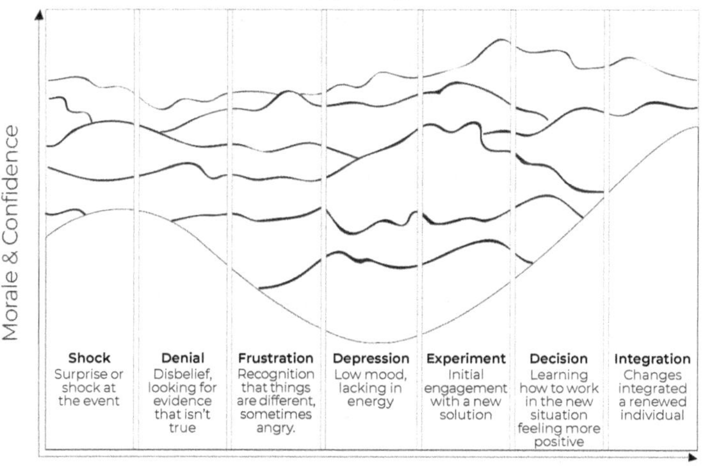

As my team moved into "decision" and "integration," what started as initial skepticism turned into telling others how to make the change journey for themselves. Talk about going from skeptic to believer! When you lead change in any part of life, it's essential to know a few things:

1. Change is emotional. Build in time for people to feel those emotions.
2. People naturally resist change. Create time to talk about that resistance.

3. Change can be managed. Get in front of it by allowing safe spaces for people to talk through their shock, denial, frustration, and depression.
4. Change is hard. Allow people to build a bridge from their emotions to their buy-in. Don't count people out just because change is hard for them. Encourage them to stay on the journey while recognizing its difficulty.
5. Know that everyone will not be able to cross the chasm with you.

Unfortunately, while your change may be taking everyone to greener pastures, some people will not be able to ride the emotions of the journey to that change. Know that this is normal and okay. Other people may opt out of being part of the team. Perhaps this change enabled them to recognize that it was time to move on. As people opt out and leave, remind yourself that new people will join and bring sincere passion for the change to propel the team forward.

Leading Change Calls for Consistency

One of the hardest things as both a leader and a human being is staying consistent. When we lead change, it's difficult, and the setbacks are often tremendous. As leaders, we may experience our own change curve as we make bold moves that are usually met with resistance. Let's not downplay how hard it is for leaders to swim against the current. After all, wouldn't it be easier to do what everyone else is doing?

Part of change is creating consistency. Be consistent with your attitude, your speech, and your transparency. Let the team know when you are experiencing a setback. Invite them to help you solve the problem. Let them see that while every ounce of your being believes in the work, you are not a superhero. Choose the right place at the right time with the right people, but be vulnerable. When a leader is truly honest about their thoughts and feelings, it creates camaraderie. People want to follow a leader who is real. Keep your true north in front of you always. It's a vision and a picture of the future that you want to build!

TAKE ACTION:

1. What is your organization's current CMMI level? What are some key things you need to do to increase your maturity level?
2. What change programs do you need to begin within your organization?
3. Instead of just forcing change, how can you plan for effective change?

FRAMEWORKS:

- CMMI—Capability Maturity Model Integration
- Change Management Vision Exercise
- Kübler-Ross Change Curve

Chapter 6

THE PRODUCT DEVELOPMENT FRAMEWORK

"If I had asked people what they wanted, they would have said faster horses."

—HENRY FORD[23]

One of the organizations I worked for loved to surface new ideas in several different ways. Some of those ways were through business plan competitions, hackathons, and the normal product development process. Each one unlocked something different and uniquely innovative in the organization. Whether methodical in its approach to innovation or wild, while staying up all night, both ways had valid reasons for existing within our ecosystem.

23 Patrick Vasklovits, "Henry Ford, Innovation, and That 'Faster Horse' Quote," *Harvard Business Review*, 29 Aug. 2011, https://hbr.org/2011/08/henry-ford-never-said-the-fast.

BUSINESS PLAN COMPETITION

For the business plan competition, one year I decided to pair up with a partner and work on a joint idea. This was an idea that I had in my head but didn't know how to design on paper. My partner was a developer and could handle some design, so he took those pieces. We had multiple pitch phases we had to get through. Our goal was to go all the way to the final showdown in Kohler, Wisconsin.

Phase 1: The Submission

Everyone that submitted an initial idea had two people they were assigned to. Those two people could take between twenty to thirty submissions for their area. However, only one person from those submissions would move on. The coaches that were assigned to those people had the job of picking the best five ideas to hear out. Here's what everyone was asked on their submission forms:

1. What is the business concept and its market need?
2. How would the idea be strategically aligned with our company?
3. Who is the target market for this product or service?
4. What is the current size and growth rate of the market?
5. Who are the competitors, and how does your offering differ from theirs?
6. What are the barriers to entry in the market?
7. What is your sales strategy?
8. What is your marketing strategy?
9. What are your assumptions around revenue, direct expense, headcount, etc.?
10. Include your financial statements for the first twelve months.

Here's what's powerful about this exercise: if even 15 percent of your organization participates in this line of thinking, you are creating a bench of business-minded innovators who are beginning to think outside of the box. Before this moment, they were only focused on their world. Now, you're asking them to think about products, the market, and the competitor. You're asking them to think strategically and—as I mentioned in chapter 1—as Dr. Stephen R. Covey would say, "Begin with the end in mind."[24] They are calculating things like EBITDA (earnings before interest tax debt and amortization) and operating expenses. In essence, you've now launched a mini-MBA course.

Phase 2: The Coaches Pitch

Now that the coaches had narrowed it down to their top six, they had their finalists turn that business plan submission into a presentation. Each team pitched its idea, and the coaches narrowed down the finalists to the one submission they wanted to move forward. Our team was ready to go. We were excited to pitch the idea that we believed in wholeheartedly. The pitch didn't last long—about twenty-five minutes, but in a few days, we received the news that we had been selected to move forward!

Phase 3: The Coaching Phase

At this point, our coach was backing our idea. Their job was to help us succeed and win the competition. Here's what was effective: we had more people thinking about the idea and the problem we were

24 Stephen R. Covey, *The 7 Habits of Highly Effective People*.

trying to solve. Their role was to tell us if we needed to speak to more customers to expose where we needed more research or design. The coach helped us develop our idea because they wanted their team to win! After several test runs, it was time to hop on a plane for the big competition.

Phase 4: The Big Huge Presentation

The top six teams selected out of all forty flew to a nice resort. This was the moment of truth. The coaches had been working with their teams for several weeks. We were up against stiff competitors who wanted the same thing we wanted.

1. **The Prize**—The winner got $50,000.
2. **The Role**—The winner got to quit their day job and run this new idea.
3. **The Win**—Let's not forget how good winning feels!

I must have stayed up all night practicing my presentation. Everyone else was at the cocktail party, and I was in my room practicing. This was my big moment. I wasn't going to spend the night socializing. I didn't get to watch anyone else's presentation, but when it was my turn, I was called to speak. The audience consisted of about thirty to forty senior leaders. They would be voting on the ideas.

I started the presentation. I was super nervous but felt like I was really driving my points home and making an impact with what I was saying. Then the unthinkable happened. When it was time to hand off the presentation to my partner, my hand hit the elaborate presentation board in front of me. It turned off the projector, and the projector screen began to roll up. Mortified, my face turned red, and moments felt like hours as my partner and I stood there trying to get the projector back on. At one point, someone came to help, but I can't remember who it was because it was like I was operating out of body. *Did I just blow it?*

We were able to get the projector back on, but we never did get the projector screen to roll back down. So we just stood there with a now fuzzy presentation projecting directly onto the wall. And that, my friends, is how you ruin what was an awesome presentation.

Needless to say, we didn't win that day. Honestly, I felt like there were several reasons:

1. **Presentation flow**—Looking back, I wish I could have tested the technology the night before. I don't think anyone could have saved the botched momentum of that presentation—at least, I couldn't.
2. **Prototype with sales**—The guy who won didn't just talk to customers; he brought a prototype and showed that he had already sold a few. He also ran a sales office for our company, so that was a very nice touch.
3. **Cocktail hour**—I should have practiced a tad less and mingled a lot more. It's not all about what you know; it's also about whom you know. Often, the deal is done before anyone has ever gotten to the table.

That day, my partner and I walked away with the door prize of $10,000 split two ways. So it wasn't a total loss, and it was a huge learning experience. I loved the adventure and the process, but the funniest part of the whole thing was that I didn't have long to lick my wounds and feel sorry for myself because guess who had to work on the winner's idea? Yes, me! I was the product development director who received the pleasure of having to work on the idea that beat me out. Poetic!

I loved the entire process because the company put as much—if not more—skin in the game as the person pitching the idea. People worked hard to go as far as they could to prove their idea had value. It was a huge win for both parties.

HACKATHONS

In addition to amazing business plan competitions, we had the phenomenon of the hackathon. This was when the technology team could work on any problem they wanted to solve within our ecosystem. Armed with Red Bull and pizza, they would stay up through the night to solve problems in record time.

Fast Teams

The teammates would partner with team members that had different skill sets than they did. A backend engineer would partner with the frontend engineer and UI/UX designer, for example. Just by forming these teams, we could see powerful innovation principles on display.

Innovation Principle: Diversity of teams in terms of thinking, approach, and problem-solving is the undercurrent that forges innovation.

Fast teams formed, silos were broken, and innovations emerged. This type of teaming is powerful and healthy.

Presenting the Prototype

The next day, a group of between twenty and thirty people would be ready to learn about the solutions the development teams created as they previewed live demos of what the teams had built overnight. Their goal was to create an MVP (minimal viable product) that could be used to solve a customer's problem.

The Winners' Circle

We would choose our top three winners, and they not only got money and bragging rights but the chance to continue to work on this problem for the next several months.

Applying Rapid Innovation

This type of event doesn't just have to be for developers. We can use these innovation concepts across any area in which we are trying to solve a problem. If there's a difficult process to solve or a solution you want to land on, this is the type of rapid prototyping you can use to surface real innovation with real results. Forcing people out of their comfort zones and into groups with those they don't usually work with sparks new ways of thinking and working.

CUSTOMER INCUBATION

One of the most engaging ways to get product and service ideas is to do an all-day incubation with some of your key customers. They can come into your office, or you can even take them off-site. Spend the day either pitching ideas to them or, even better, letting them pitch ideas to you.

I have done customer competitions where the best idea wins a prize. You'd be surprised how competitive your customers get when winning is on the line (or maybe you're not surprised at all). Make it annual, and invite only a select few. Your customers will ask you how they can get invited to this incubation session.

STRATEGIC PLANNING (INTEGRATED PLANS)

Another more traditional way to surface ideas is via strategic planning cycles. The goal of these sessions is to look into the future, think about where the market and customer are going, and plan to meet them there. The most important word in the whole equation is strategy. So, what's the strategy for the next one to three years? Your team should build this together and create an integrated plan that traverses the whole organization. How will each team own their piece of the integrated plan?

Typically, to facilitate this, it would occur over a couple of days and potentially off-site. The teams bring their top three key strategies to designate their playing field and how they will win on that playing field. The goal of the rest of the team is to ask questions and really dig into their approach and pressure test it. In reviewing all of the business cases, the team is prepared to rank and prioritize them. From there, we may do some additional market research, landing on which ideas are most likely to take flight.

INNOVATION COMES FROM EVERYWHERE

Innovation can be both "bottom-up" and "top-down." From the top, by putting these types of controls in place, we can see how the organization can sustain innovation but have the right triggers in place and create a strong foundation for teams to build on. No matter where your organization finds itself on the maturity index, these ideas should help you begin to lean into innovation.

SIMPLE PRODUCT DEVELOPMENT FRAMEWORK

Start to create a product development process by following this simple framework:

1. **Team up**—Pull together a cross-functional team. Begin to whiteboard and map out the process.
2. **Test out**—Test the process by trying it on a very small innovation project. Where do you need to adjust? What could make it better? What did not work? Document all of these things. Iterate by improving the process as many times as you can until you have a working solution.
3. **Pitch it**—Pitch the process to your team or senior leaders. If you don't have their buy-in, the process will never work, and your innovations will not see the light of day. Walk them through the test you ran, be honest about what worked and what didn't, and show them how your iterations improved the process over time. Show the benefits of collaboration and the cost savings of getting all teams in alignment early.

4. **Adjust it**—Based on the feedback you've received from senior leaders, get your team back together and adjust it. Processes should be iterative which means they never get old; they always evolve and change as you learn. Version out your process so that as you change it, you can speak to what version of the process you are on.
5. **Try it**—Now you are ready to try it on a larger scale product design. Stay close to the learnings, so you can share them in real time and continue to adjust the process as you learn.

What Should Be in a Framework

Your framework should contain how to surface ideas throughout the organization and how to rank them and decipher the appetite to test them out. Once tested, how do we measure success? How do we measure failure? How do we learn from that failure?

If you can start to articulate those things, you are on your way to a simple product development process.

- Intake Ideas
- Surface Good Ideas
- Test Ideas
- Frame How to Invest in Good Ideas—"What makes an idea good?"
- Measure Success
- Surface Learnings
- Launch Ideas

Each phase will have inputs, outputs, and clear decision-makers to ensure the process moves forward.

IDEATION

Intaking Ideas

How do good ideas get into your organization? Business plan contests, pitching ideas to senior leaders, customer listening sessions, hackathons, carrier pigeons, suggestion boxes—no matter how—you must find a way to surface *good* ideas and see if they can be turned into *great* ideas.

Surfacing Ideas

You will quickly find there is no shortage of good ideas. So how do you surface the ones you want to work on? There needs to be a rapid process to vet ideas and quickly weigh the ideas you want to work on. I love it when team members come to me in this phase and say, "I have already spoken to twenty customers who seem excited about this idea," or better yet, "I have ten purchase orders for customers that will buy this if we build it." Those are the types of ideas I am willing to test. It's not about lobbing ideas over the fence to make someone else do the leg work. It's about showing that the idea already has legs. Those are the ideas that leaders are more likely to invest in and work on.

Testing and Measuring Ideas

Ideas must be tested. It saves us time and money when we test. This seems like common sense, but you'd be surprised at the number of product and feature ideas launched because the founder thought it was a great idea. Teams must feel empowered to test every and all good ideas—no matter who suggested them. Built into our test, needs to be a way to measure how the test went. To decide if we should move forward to invest in an idea, it has to have three things:

1. **Ubiquity**—It solves a problem for many customers, not just one.
2. **Funding**—Will customers buy this, or do they think of it as more of a feature?
3. **Urgency**—Customers are ready to buy it now.

PROTOTYPE

Investing in the Concept

Once we have hit these three levers, it's time to decide how much we will invest in the concept by building a prototype. This is essentially another round of testing: Testing 2.0. We still haven't committed to going all in, but we are mitigating our risk from idea to full investment by creating a prototype. We will take this prototype back to the customers we originally spoke to as well as a few new ones to see what they think. Does it still hit the three levers of ubiquity, funding, and urgency?

This will serve as another go-no-go stage-gate. Expect that 70-80 percent of your ideas will not make it out of the concept phase, or they will be kicked back to the idea phase for more work.

Iterating on the Concept

At each of these phases, we need to ask hard questions about the usability of the concept. This may not be a one-time thing; you may need to iterate through these phases several times before you launch. It's not about perfection. Something a former CEO of mine used to say was "80 percent of the need for 80 percent of the market." So it doesn't have to be perfect, but it does need to hit the vein of the core need. If it's not hitting that vein, or if it's only resonating with half of the customers, you need to refine your offering until it resonates with more.

Measuring Success

Before developing the concept, it needs to be asked, "How will success be measured when the product is launched?" It is imperative to know this beforehand. There are many different ways to measure success, but you must ask, "How does *our* organization truly measure success?" If you can measure all your product launches using similar metrics, then you can start to create some baselines to understand why something was successful or why it was not. Here are some of the ways to measure product success—consider building a scorecard from these.

- The number of customers that preorder your product
- Percentage of customers that adopt the product through usage
- Percentage of market share impact
- Percentage of customer retention
- Win rate over competitors
- Revenue numbers
- Customer feedback

Here are two examples of how you could use metrics to assess your success.

The number of customers who preorder your product:

- Campaign Timeline: August 1, 2023 through December 1, 2023
- Number of total customers: 1,000
- Goal: 150 customer preorders
- Actual: 250 customer preorders
- Success Rate based on Goal: 167 percent rate of success
- Methods Used: We trained customer success teams to talk about the product as a part of the account review with their customers. We believed that 15 percent of customers would express interest. We were surprised to see that 25 percent of customers expressed an interest when provided with an opportunity to buy.

The percentage of customers who adopt the product through usage:

- Campaign Timeline: January 3, 2024 through March 3, 2024
- Goal: 120 customers
- Actual: 35 customers
- Success Rate: 29 percent rate of success
- Methods Used: We tried a test where we educated only the southeast inside sales team to sell this product. In order to reach our desired adoption rate, we should have trained all four teams. Training to pitch this product takes between two and three months. By cutting the number of teams we trained, we did not reach our goal of 120 customers.

Create a scorecard, and really understand why the product test succeeded or failed.

DEVELOPMENT

We are now reaching another go-no-go stage-gate. Based on the feedback we've received from our customers, should we move forward into development? If the answer is "yes," our goal should still be to release features iteratively. We want to provide as much value for the customer as fast as possible through these iterative releases. Let them begin getting value early and providing you with early feedback.

Surface Learnings

As the customer begins to use the product, they will have questions and need adjustments. These will help you create a product backlog of items that can make what you are building even better. In a later chapter, we will spend more time on product launch.

TAKE ACTION:

- How can you surface ideas and innovation on your team?
- What are some ways you can create disruption in normal team dynamics to spark innovation?
- With whom could you team to create this product development framework helping the organization find clarity on how something evolves from an idea to a product?

FRAMEWORKS:

- Product Development Framework

Chapter 7

FAILURE: INNOVATION'S TRAINING GROUND

"When the winds of change blow, some people build walls and others build windmills."

—ANCIENT CHINESE PROVERB

Creating breakthrough innovation is not an easy undertaking. If it were, everyone would do it. It takes a certain team dynamic, collaboration, and overall commitment to the bigger picture of what kind of impact a breakthrough innovation could have on your organization. Innovation is arguably the biggest advantage for growth in the marketplace. While there isn't a secret formula to unlocking these transformative ideas, there are practices that enable real innovation with real results. One of the most important innovation practices I've continually seen is how an organization handles failure.

I once worked at a company where a project crashed and burned, and the outcomes were not even close to being met. I was asked to come in to facilitate a lessons-learned retrospective. I started out by saying that it's always best when we can each own what we could do differently. It's the only way to really improve. Immediately, everyone started shifting blame and accusing each other. I had to stop the session several times and ask, "What can YOU personally do differently next time?" It got really quiet; no one was willing to admit what they did wrong, but they were more than happy to throw each other under the bus. Frustrated, I realized a team like this wasn't going to learn anything because psychological safety and self-awareness were not at the helm.

This further proved to me that an environment of fear can quickly expand into an environment of groupthink and denial. There's hardly any room to grow in these environments because it is in the exploration of the "how" and "why" we failed that we're able to create new pathways for success. If we sweep our failures under the rug, no one learns, grows, or gets better. If we can unpack and highlight why we failed and what didn't work and remain inquisitive, we can move our entire team from critical to curious—a giant stepping stone to creating a culture of innovation.

Innovation Principle: We have learned more from our failures than we ever have from our successes.

FAILURE ISN'T FATAL

One of the companies with which I worked for most of my career taught me that failure wasn't fatal. But let's be clear: not all environments share this philosophy. In fact, countless workplaces and management styles emphasize the opposite: failure equals a loss of dignity and, potentially, even the loss of a job.

Do people get fired if they fail? Well, that's a problem! Teams should be taught to fail fast, fail cheap, and fail often. Sometimes failure is the only way we will truly learn to succeed. An organization's willingness to allow for failure can feel frightening, but it's all about what you do with that failure. Do you learn from it?

Leaders must take charge of spearheading these efforts. What is something you tried multiple times and failed at before success was reached? Share this with your team, and ask for their examples as well. Creating an honest environment in which people don't feel the pressure to be perfect fosters trust—which in turn fosters innovation. Sharing our failures also enables us to give and receive rapid feedback. Organizations that prioritize this are healthier and see higher revenues and returns.

The idea of failing fast and failing cheap is simply that we must place guardrails around our ideas and innovations. These guardrails keep us from going out too far, too fast. When I would build new products, I would never take a fully baked product to the customer. I would take sketches and drawings and tell them about the problems it would solve for them. Sometimes, they looked bored. Other times, they would lean in and say, "Tell me more." Once I could get at least ten customers to say, "Tell me more," I knew I was ready to go to the next phase. If I never garnered that excitement, my guardrails told me to go back to the drawing board with that idea and count it as a failure.

You will see that creating a simple product guardrails scorecard will not only prevent you from overthinking it but also help the team to slow down and learn as opposed to continuing to push an idea that is not working in the market. If I cannot get a customer to commit to buying, then it's a failure, and I need to take the time to learn. If we receive their excitement and interest, it's time to move from sketch to prototype and keep testing the idea. Sometimes, there's not enough interest, so we need to do more research or tweak some of the features that did not sit quite right.

Simple Product Guardrails Scorecard

PRODUCT	# OF CUSTOMERS IN PRODUCT TEST	# OF CUSTOMERS WILLING TO BUY	PERCENTAGE OF INTEREST	NEXT STEPS
Product A	30	1	3.3%	Fail/ Learn
Product B	25	18	72%	Pass/ Proto-type
Product C	40	9	22.5%	Needs more research

It's important to recognize that nobody goes to work hoping to feel criticized or condemned for their failed innovations, and no one sets out to fail on purpose. In turn, people tend to hide their failures when they feel they may be met with criticism.

Counting failures triggers the need to learn. Instead of hiding your failures, put them front and center and have others help you learn from them. By sharing those learnings, you make the team think more critically and deliberately about their approach to launching new ideas and initiatives. Also, by adding others to the conversation, it's like creating a board of directors around you. Each person sitting at the table can see things from an angle that you cannot.

By cultivating an encouraging environment, allowing for failure, and putting proper structure around teams and ideas, you can create a pathway to innovation within your organization. Of course, this is just the beginning of creating a culture of breakthrough innovators. When team members feel heard, they are engaged; when they are engaged, they bring their best ideas to the table.

Innovation builds excitement and engagement within an organization. Learning how to help teams rise from failure and move forward with confidence is a key component of leadership. With a culture and mindset that each loss carries a valuable lesson, everyone wins. If it's done right, failure is not fatal! In fact, Thomas Edison is often quoted (sometimes accurately, sometimes not) regarding how much effort and persistence it takes to succeed. And I love how he put it when a reporter asked him about his previous mistakes: "I have not failed 10,000 times—I've successfully found 10,000 ways that will not work."[25]

Here are a few other product failures you may remember for which the customer base didn't ask or which were not milestone-checked along the way.

Apple | The Newton | 1993

This technology was supposed to be designed for people who were not necessarily into computers. The claim was that it would change our lives as much as the cell phone or the fax machine! This was a PDA (personal digital assistant) designed with a calculator, date book, and computer. You wrote on the screen, and it would turn your writing into notes you could fax. There were calendaring and map features as well. It didn't have a keyboard; it required a stylus—about which Steve Jobs said when discussing touch screen capability, "Who wants a stylus? . . . You have to get 'em, put 'em away, you lose 'em. Yuck! Nobody wants a stylus. So let's not use a stylus."[26] It's not surprising that it was axed in 1997 when he returned to Apple. It also didn't connect you to the cellular network. Dissecting why it didn't work had to be the catalyst for many Apple inventions, including the first iPhone released in 2007.

---

25 Erica R. Hendry, "7 Epic Fails Brought to You by the Genius Mind of Thomas Edison," *Smithsonian*, 20 Nov. 2013, https://www.smithsonianmag.com/innovation/7-epic-fails-brought-to-you-by-the-genius-mind-of-thomas-edison-180947786/#:~:text=In%20response%20to%20a%20question,ways%20that%20will%20not%20work.%E2%80%9D.

26 David Goldman, "'Over My Dead Body.' The Pencil and Four Other Things Steve Jobs Would Hate," *CNNBusiness*, 10 Sept. 2015, https://money.cnn.com/2015/09/10/technology/apple-pencil-steve-jobs-stylus/index.html.

Friendster | Social Media Site | 2002

Friendster had a head start over Facebook and a ton of venture capital backing. The Friendster site was riddled with site performance issues, and website downtime became a critical issue for Friendster to tackle.[27] Friendster focused on trying to localize their site and translate it into other languages when the foundations were not in place.[28] When you don't have the basic foundations you can't build innovation on top of an unstable infrastructure. And as we know, it didn't stick around long-term. Its competitor, Facebook, came in, providing a more methodical approach to the market and quickly gained traction.

Windows Vista | 2007

Windows Vista was known as a buggy mess and was not warmly received by its users. Many machines that upgraded to Vista—and even machines with "the latest and greatest hardware"—were not powerful enough to run the new operating system.[29] New graphics with Aero made it hardware intensive, so it ran slower on computers. And there were compatibility issues with other manufacturers. Drivers would frequently crash, and permission prompts would pop up constantly. While they did try to release fixes, the damage was done.

---

27 Viktor Hendelmann, "What Happened to Friendster? 4 Reasons Why It Failed," *Productmint*, 22 Dec. 2022, https://productmint.com/what-happened-to-friendster/.
28 Todd Hoff, "Friendster Lost Lead Because of a Failure to Scale," *High Scalability*, 13 Nov. 2007, http://highscalability.com/blog/2007/11/13/friendster-lost-lead-because-of-a-failure-to-scale.html.
29 Nithil Krishnaraj, "Windows Vista: Why Did It Fail?" *Medium*, 22 June 2020, https://medium.com/techtalkers/windows-vista-why-did-it-fail-b3ba4bd08a74.

Facebook Home | 2013

The Facebook Home Android app didn't get much traction in the marketplace as it didn't give you the ease to toggle between your phone and its Facebook news feed. Overall a lack of customization options and other issues ruled it out as a contender.

Google Glass | 2013

These were designed to be wearable tech that had smartphone capabilities like making calls, taking photos and videos, and checking your social media. After two years on the market, consumers were neither asking for nor did they need Google Glass. This tech was riddled with issues like low battery life, bugs, and privacy issues, and the price for select "Glass Explorers" was sky-high at $1500.[30] At the end of the day, one of *TIME* magazine's "Best Inventions of the Year" just didn't measure up.[31]

Why Did It Fail?

What all of these ideas have in common is that the failures were expensive and took place over long periods of time. We should always be asking questions:

- How do we avoid a slow-moving trainwreck where we spend a ton of money with very little to show for it?
- How can I stay so aligned with my customer or end user that I am creating things that drive customer delight?

30 Nick Bilton, "Why Google Glass Broke," *The New York Times*, 4 Feb. 2015, https://www.nytimes.com/2015/02/05/style/why-google-glass-broke.html.
31 "Best Inventions of the Year 2012," *Time*, 31 Oct. 2012, https://techland.time.com/2012/11/01/best-inventions-of-the-year-2012/slide/google-glass/.

- How can I build things they want (pull), not things I want them to have (push)?

When something is pushed on the market, it usually doesn't fare well.

I can't leave my own stories out of these scenarios. I worked in a tech company early in my career, and we had many products we tried out that didn't work. We tried to build a professional network like LinkedIn. We didn't have the name recognition or traction. Only our company and our friends joined, and it never really took hold in the market.

We also tried to build a job referral engine into an app that leveraged social media to provide job recommendations to your friends. At that time, the idea of combining job search and social media was a little taboo. The idea didn't really take off the way we had hoped. Well, it didn't take off at all.

All of these ideas were things the market didn't ask us for but things we hoped they needed. We went all the way into development before we verified there was a real need. A simple sketch or prototype may have told us there was no market for our product.

When we are on a healthy team, we allow for safe failures with stage-gates, so we don't get too far into developing products that no one wants. We learn from our failures and bounce back quickly. So, lean into small failures and treat them as learnings. Those learnings help you launch whatever it is you desire to build.

Exercises for Generation of Ideas

Allow teams to start small by giving them a three-week sprint to generate small hypotheses around some key features or product ideas. Sketch them out, do some light research, and test them with customers or users. Have them come back and share what resonated and what didn't resonate with the customer. The person who has the most failed hypotheses gets celebrated. Why? Because they were willing to test, fail, and admit failure. We are celebrating three things:

1. They moved their ego out of the way and admitted the failure.
2. They tested their work when it was cheap and small versus large and visible.
3. We, as the leaders, are showing them it's safe to fail and learn from that.

FAILURE VS. MISTAKES—FAILING FORWARD

When hiring, I really look for people who have experienced failure and recovered. It's not just whether or not the person has failed. It's also if they are willing to share that failure with others. This shows that not only have they learned from it, but they don't have so much ego that they can't talk about it. Much of failure is in the resiliency to get back up and show the tenaciousness to try again.

Often when I work on projects with team members, there is a breaking point. Some people throw their hands up in the air because it has gotten too hard. They might mentally check out or—worse—physically check out. But others dig in and keep trying. It's all too easy to tap out when things get hard, but past failure allows us to understand that if we keep pressing through, there are answers on the other side. We should be trying new things constantly. If we are doing that, some things will not work out. That truth can't become detrimental. Instead, it has to propel us forward to try the next thing.

Mistakes

Having a hypothesis and trying it is different than making a mistake. We want to learn and grow from mistakes, but those are different from failures. Once we make a mistake, our goal should be not to make that same mistake again. Making the same mistake continuously is showing our inability to retain that information or, perhaps, even incompetence in a certain area. So we separate those two words in our minds. They're different and should be treated differently.

Here are a few hiring questions you can ask to see how team members have handled failure in the past:

1. When was the last time you failed, and what type of project were you working on?
2. Why did it fail, and what did you do to overcome the challenge?
3. Who worked with you on that team, and who led the project?
4. What was their contribution or role, and what was yours?
5. What did you disagree about when forming your hypothesis?
6. How did you eventually solve those disagreements?
7. Did you vocalize those disagreements or just think them to yourself?
8. How did the team rise after the failure?
9. What were the end results of the project?

In product development, you will have many versions of ideas until you get to the idea that actually sticks. You know—the one the customer loves and beats down your door to pay for. That's the one that matters. And you will only arrive at those types of solutions if you are willing to fail on version 1.0, version 2.0, version 3.0 . . . until you get to version 10.0 that you know the customer will love.

In life and in business, we have to know how to fail and how to fall. When you are learning a sport like martial arts, one of the first things they teach you is how to fall and how to get back up. We do our teams a disservice when we don't teach people how to do the same in business and leadership. Otherwise, we create leaders and teams that are too afraid to innovate and too afraid to launch new things.

In other words, the fear of not creating something new has to be greater than the fear of failing at it. But that can't be done alone. It has to be done with a team of people who are willing to take risks—a team of people who are willing to fail. We fail and fall together, and then we rise together. That's the kind of team I want to work with. We will fail fast, fail cheap, and rise smarter.

The ultimate team member is:

- Talented
- Self-aware
- Willing to take risks
- Quick to learn from failure (because it triggers learning)

TAKE ACTION:

- What is your organization's stance on failure?
- When was the last time that you failed? How was that failure handled by you and by others?
- Have you ever thought about ensuring you hire someone who has failed before?
- How can you help your team understand that failure is not fatal if they are willing to learn?

FRAMEWORKS:

- Guardrails
- Idea Generation

Chapter 8

HUMAN-CENTERED DESIGN AND VISUAL AGREEMENT

"The human brain can process images up to 60,000 times faster than text."

—REBEKAH CARTER[32]

I was brought in to serve a client that had a lot of miscommunication and rework internally. I asked if I could begin to sit in and observe their meetings to get a sense of what was going on. I instantly noticed three things that were deeply hurting the client's cause.

1) They hadn't assigned roles in the meeting.
   - Assign a person to take notes.
   - Assign someone to keep time.
   - Assign someone to facilitate the meeting.

---

32 Rebekah Carter, "25 Key Graphic Design Statistics & Facts to Know in 2023," *Findstack*, 6 Sept. 2022, https://findstack.com/resources/graphic-design-statistics/.

Since roles were not understood or assigned, most people checked out during the meeting because they felt they had no part to play. They were on laptops and phones because large chunks of the meeting did not apply to them.

Consider This: *If you want to know if someone is taking your meeting seriously, observe the number of side conversations they decide to participate in.*

Often, people have side conversations for two reasons: It's a poorly run meeting, and they are bored. They are not being heard, so they need to share their thoughts with their neighbor. When side conversations occur, we need to get curious. We need to ask, "What are we missing from this conversation that you'd like to add?"

2) They weren't working visually.

- Working visually allows us to do more than just talk; it allows us to see what you mean.
- Drawing and writing on the board help us get visual agreement on what we just covered.

No matter whether the meeting is on Zoom or in person, the ability to capture everyone's ideas visually does a few things. First, it lets people feel heard. If they do not feel heard, it will lengthen the meeting as they figure out different ways to say the same thing. When we capture their thoughts, it allows us to not only refer to their ideas later but also help them to know that they were heard.

Capturing visually allows people who are late to the meeting to visually catch up by reviewing what has already been captured in notes or on the board. Nothing is worse than needing to recap the meeting every time a new person walks in late. Visual notes allow you to continue to move forward because everyone has already seen this movie. They don't want to keep rewinding.

3) They didn't follow up or follow through.

- Clarify decisions vs. opinions to define next steps.
- Decide who owns it.
- Send out action items.

In this meeting, I noticed that they talked in circles. People made statements, and it was unclear if those statements were decisions or someone's opinion. What about the next steps and who owns it? Their meetings were frustrating and not productive, and there was no sense of forward momentum after you left the room. People yelled some things out in the chaos, but you weren't sure if they were heard by anyone.

If we treated that meeting as human-centered, we would design the meeting for the people in the room. They are busy executives, and they don't have a lot of time on their hands. The last thing they have time to do is sit through an unproductive meeting. When we start to see things through a human-centered lens, everything changes. This meeting was frustrating, and the attendees weren't getting anything done. But what if the meeting could be fun and effective instead?

A 2018 Salary.com survey reports, "Each day in the U.S. there are at least 36 million meetings that waste about $37 billion in lost productivity. [Meetings can be a waste of money because] workers daydream (91%), do other work that has nothing to do with the meeting (73%), feel overwhelmed by the number of meetings they have to attend (45%), sleep (39%) and respond to emails or texts (31%)."[33]

Innovation Principle: Meeting culture is a reflection of company culture.

If meeting culture is a direct reflection of company culture, we have some work to do in organizations if we want to run fun and effective meetings.

The first thing I asked them to do was think about their meetings in three buckets:

- Preparing for the meeting
- Hosting the meeting
- Following up after the meeting

PREPARING FOR THE MEETING

I asked the team to begin thinking like facilitators. Facilitators don't just come into a room cold; they think about their audience by:

- Preparing an agenda.
- Thinking through the logistics. (How does the room need to be set up?)

33 Dan Schawbel, "Why Most Meetings Are a Waste and How to Have an Effective One," LinkedIn, 16 Dec. 2019, https://www.linkedin.com/pulse/why-most-meetings-waste-how-have-effective-one-dan-schawbel/.

- Considering hybrid. (Will there be people online and in the room? What's the best experience?)
- Creating a facilitation guide that gives the amount of time they want to spend on each topic.
- Sending data and pre-reads in advance.
- Starting and ending the meeting on time.
- Assigning meeting roles.

HOSTING THE MEETING

When hosting, I asked the team to start the meeting by telling everyone what they would be talking about and for how long. In the meeting, we will:

- State goals of what brought us together.
- Explain the outcomes we'd like to accomplish before we leave.
- Time box every topic.
- Work visually on the board or through tools like MURAL (similar to an online whiteboard).
- Drive toward next steps and key decisions.

I told this team to practice getting their ideas out and up on a board where all could visually see them. Sometimes, the most innovative ideas are buried, and they have to be surfaced. They also needed to slow their conversations down, so they could hear from other voices in the room. Frequently, the talkers were drowning out the others in the room. Five voices of twelve were being heard. Having someone facilitate the conversation and look for times to help the room pause and hear what others had to say is key.

FOLLOWING UP AFTER THE MEETING

After the meeting ends, the work isn't over. Now it's time to follow up and follow through on what happened in the meeting.

- Send out notes between twenty-four and forty-eight hours after the meeting.
- Owners and due dates—Who owns each action item, and by when is a follow-up due?
- Follow up and follow through—Since you scheduled the meeting, it's up to you to ensure participants close all loops from the meeting. Let's not drop the ball on any action items.

It may sound odd, but running better meetings helps us innovate. It saves us time, money, and effort. When we run bad meetings, it demotivates and disenfranchises the people who have to sit through them. Running better meetings is part of being an effective leader.

COLLABORATION AND INNOVATION

How can we foster rapid innovation and collaboration within our meetings, when pitching ideas, or for creating products?

We need to think human first and, as a result, visually. If we are constantly asking ourselves, *How can I show this visually? How can I explain this visually?* then that puts us in a good place to ensure what we are explaining is properly understood.

Have you ever been in a meeting with several people, and you only spoke verbally and wrote nothing down? After leaving the meeting, there was no real follow-up. When you came back together to meet again, half of the room couldn't remember what you talked about. The other half of the room went off to execute the ideas, but when they brought the ideas back together, it felt like you were all in different rooms.

Visual agreement is the most underutilized meeting superpower. Visual agreement helps us gain clarity and make decisions faster. Lack of visual agreement is the lazy way to run a meeting. Yes, it's easier in the short term, but it's always more difficult in the longer term. Failure to document the thoughts, actions, and decisions necessary to be effective creates misunderstandings later on. Leveraging visual agreement allows us to do the work now, so we don't have to wade through misunderstandings later. Visual agreement also helps us to work in the meeting instead of talking about the work we need to do when we leave the meeting.

If you are looking to save time, ensure that you are not scheduling meetings that should be emails and sending emails that should be meetings.

Emails should be triggered when:

- It's a one-way conversation (informational).
- You need to get information out quickly.
- The decision is already made.
- There's not a ton of room for discussion or questions.
- The issue is simple (not complex).

Meetings should be triggered when:

- There's a need for collaboration with important stakeholders.
- The right direction is unclear, and there's a need to generate ideas and options.

- The issue is complex, with several moving pieces or parts, and you need all the right stakeholders at the table to make key decisions.
- You are creating something new or changing something critical.
- Delivering a training or presenting educational material.
- Delivering transformational or change-based information.
- You need visual agreement with what you are building and creating.

Here's another example of visual agreement in practice—the ability to show how your idea works by getting it out of your head and on the board and allowing people to ask questions.

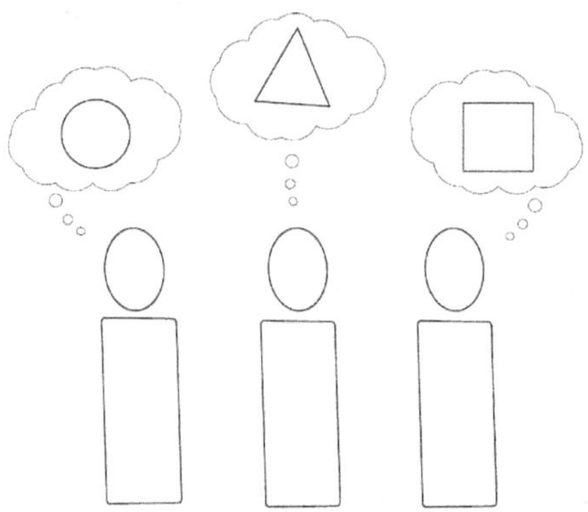

I'm glad we all agree!

This picture beautifully depicts something in the top left. They all think they mean the same thing.

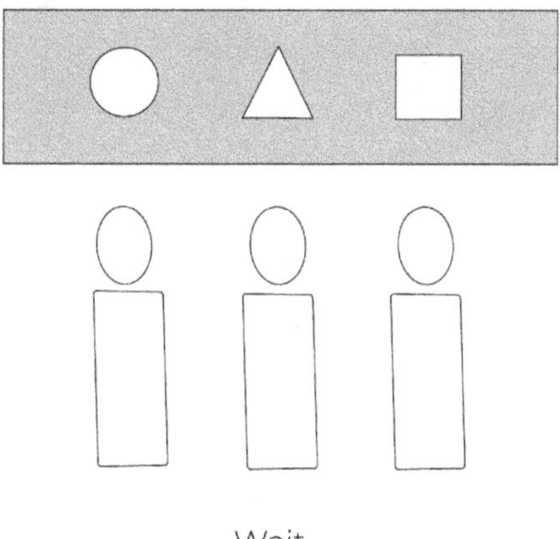

Wait...

However, upon writing it down, they realize that they are all, in fact, thinking something different.

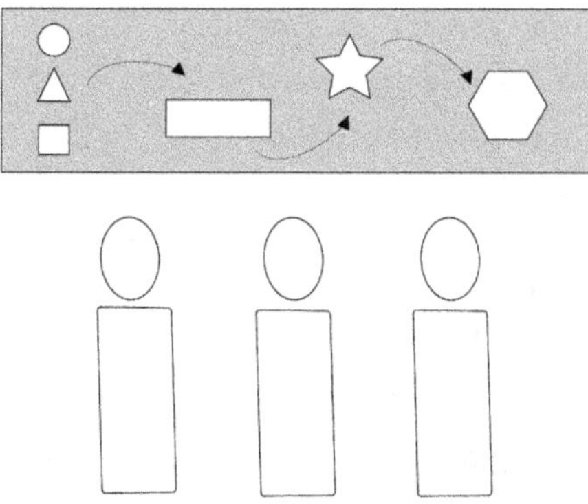

That's more like it!

Then they build on the idea to take and shape that idea into something better. *Now* they are all on the same page.

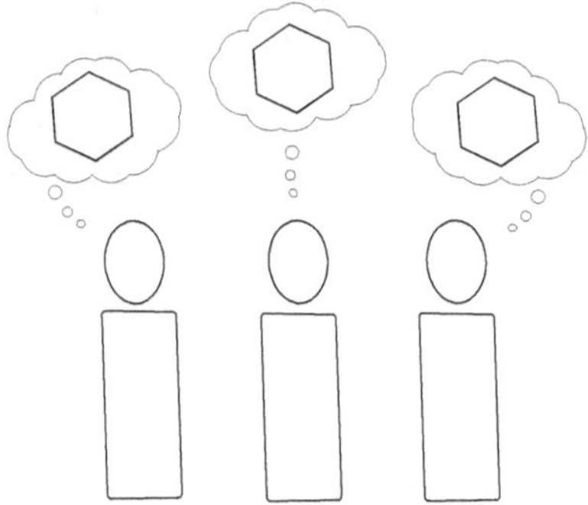

Now we all agree!

The dynamic shifts from "That will never work" to asking questions like:

- What did you have in mind?
- How would you solve this problem?
- What would need to be true for this to work?
- I think this could work if. . . .

See what happens? We instantly shift our brains from "no" to "What if?" We shift our brains from no to a different ethos, one that says, "Let's test. Let's explore. Let's understand."

WHAT GIVES RISE TO INNOVATION?

We can start by capturing everyone's ideas on the board or on sticky notes. This does two things: It gets both good and bad ideas out there.

It allows others to build on the ideas present. Rather than hide our crazy ideas, we get them all out there right in the open.

According to the University of Minnesota, the human brain can process images up to 60,000 times faster than text. What's more, 90% of the information transmitted to the brain from the world around us is visual.[34] Therefore, I am going to give you a simple way to do this. It's called open, explore, and close.

OPEN, EXPLORE, AND CLOSE

In my experience, most people struggle in one of these three areas:

1. **Open**—How to open a collaborative conversation where we look at every idea.
2. **Explore**—How to group like ideas together and then inspect what good ideas will work well.
3. **Close**—How to close ideation and discussion. The importance of this phase is helping to drive toward a key decision.

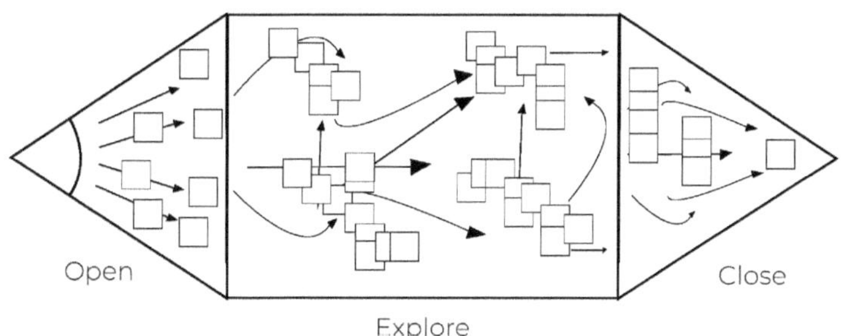

34 Rebekah Carter, "25 Key Graphic Design Statistics & Facts to Know in 2023."

Open

Opening allows you to put as many ideas on the board as you possibly can without holding back.

When you are trying to solve a problem or name a highly visible marketing project, you can get started by generating as many ideas as possible. Once each member of the team has generated ten ideas, let's talk about them (not shoot them down or pop balloons). We want to spark even more thoughts around the topic. You can do this two or three times until you feel everyone has run out of ideas.

Open

Explore

Now it's time to move into exploring. Once we surface those ideas, we try to group like ideas. We call this affinity mapping. On the surface, it may look like we have forty ideas, but when we group ideas or concepts together, we really have ten main ideas. Narrow them down, and vote on the ideas to see which people like the best. This voting helps people detach from their own ideas and see the bigger landscape of possibilities. Once everyone's voted, tally the scores.

Close

Here's where most people tend to struggle—the when and how of closing ideation. Ideation must come to an end by making some core decisions. We have three ideas, but we need to narrow those down to one good idea that we want the team to run with.

Let's break the teams up into small groups. Create three teams and give each one of the ideas. Have them go off for thirty minutes together and really flesh out the idea. Have them pitch the idea back to the group. Now it's time to decide. You can have one final

Close

decision-maker in the room, or you can do it as a team, but the most important part of innovation is to drive toward a decision, so the team can execute the vision.

Does It Seem Odd?

For some, this type of collaboration feels odd. Why jump through all the hoops when I could have just made the decision on my own in the first five minutes? This type of exercise teaches teams three things:

1. How to work together.
2. How to rapidly generate ideas.
3. How to pitch their ideas with clarity.

Having ten people who know how to do this on a team creates a bench of innovators as opposed to having one person always be the "idea guy." When we develop and invest in people's ideas, they show up differently to work. They show up like an owner—not a renter. They show up ready to innovate.

TAKE ACTION:

- What is your meeting culture like?
- What are one or two changes you could make right away?
- How could you adapt the Open, Explore, Close framework to more meetings?
- What are some ways you can adopt working visually?

FRAMEWORK:

- Open, Explore, Close
- Visual Thinking

Chapter 9
INNOVATION FUNDING AND FRAMEWORKS

"Successful innovators use an 'innovation pyramid,' with several big bets at the top that get most of the investment; a portfolio of promising midrange ideas in test stage; and a broad base of early stage ideas or incremental innovations. Ideas and influence can flow up or down the pyramid."

—CARMEN NOBEL, HARVARD BUSINESS SCHOOL[35]

While working for a large multinational, I realized that there were several projects limping along, but a really high-profile project was failing. In the chapter on failure, we covered how important it is to learn from our failures. It's equally as important to learn from the failures of others. One day, I was reading a *Harvard Business Review*

35 Carmen Nobel, "Funding Innovation: Is Your Firm Doing It Wrong?" *HBS Working Knowledge*, 19 Sept. 2012, https://hbswk.hbs.edu/item/funding-innovation-is-your-firm-doing-it-wrong.

article called "Funding Innovation: Is Your Firm Doing it Wrong?" I had an "Aha!" moment.

In this article, Carmen Nobel told a cautionary tale about innovation. What I saw in this article that began to ring true is that not only must ideas, features, and products have stage-gates to ensure their success but also to ensure the bright idea doesn't later lead to our downfall.

Nokia and Apple took center stage in this storyline, and it paralleled with a large program my organization was working on at the time. This project was sucking millions of dollars out of the organization. It was so big and unwieldy it didn't seem like any leader could wrestle it to the ground. In fact, the leaders working on this project became a revolving door. When I began to read this article, I realized that we were also doing it wrong.

According to the article, Nokia consistently outspent Apple on phone-related research and development over a ten-year period. For example, between 2004 and 2007, before the iPhone's release, Nokia spent roughly $22 billion in R&D compared to Apple's $2.5 billion. When the first iPhone launched in 2007 it outperformed Nokia's offering in terms of profit margin. Since that launch, Apple has continued to far outperform Nokia in terms of both its profit margins and its reputation for innovation. So what gives?

> *"This was a slow-moving train wreck," Professor Josh Lerner said. "There was a sense that the key innovations developed during the war, like radar and the atomic bomb, came from a very scientific-driven process. So, corporations made*

enormous investments to create ivory towers where scientists would think great thoughts."[36]

So, big dollars but no big returns? Organizations can't afford to operate this way anymore. In fact, it's part of the reason why innovation is not always a nice word in some organizations. It feels like there are no boundaries, high spending, and little return. If we are going to innovate properly, we must change this. We must set it on fire. The old way of doing things is not working. We need to thrust teams out of their chairs and into the world of their customer.

Innovation Principle: We must set it on fire. The old way of doing things is not working.

As we build any innovation program, we have to continue to ask, "Does this satisfy the needs of my customer NOW?" Now is an important word because the target is constantly changing. Some people create a persona once and then set it and forget it. Your persona should be updated often (at the least, review every eighteen months) because wants, needs, and desires are directly tied to your return on investment.

INNOVATION IS FREEDOM WITHIN A FRAMEWORK

Oftentimes, boundaries—not endless pools of money—are what help us innovate. Giving people a framework or boundaries actually allows them to focus their research, time, and intentions on a finite number

36 Carmen Nobel, "Funding Innovation: Is Your Firm Doing It Wrong?"

of directions, not infinite. Don't just sit down and try to think about ideas. Think about a problem and how you can solve it. People cannot solve problems they don't know about. For most people, innovation starts with a problem statement. So start with the problem you are trying to solve, look at the resources you have to solve it, and start there. That's innovation.

Create a framework for teams within your organization to use. Where there's a lack of framework or clarity, people make it up. The leader's job is to give their team stable frameworks to build on. Your stable framework is like building a house, and the foundational layer—what we talked about in chapter 1— is your vision, mission, values, and goals. These things inform your culture and drive your behaviors.

How can we think about funding innovation programs that don't break the bank? Here are some guiding principles of how we should think about funding innovation.

FUNDING: NEW PRODUCTS AND SERVICES

A good test for whether or not innovation is happening is to ask yourself if your company has released a new product or service in the last three years that equates to at least 15 percent of the overall revenue. If you are not releasing new products and services, you're not planning for future growth. If you are not planning for future growth, you are planning to not be around. At the core, we should be listening, testing, and prototyping new ideas constantly. Don't just invest in today. Invest in the future.

Does your company have a line-item designation or department that focuses on innovation? I believe innovation should be owned by everyone in the company. Earlier, we talked about some ways that could happen, but research and development or innovation should be planned and budgeted for.

INNOVATION PORTFOLIOS

You will have different levels of portfolio risk, but all of those innovations should be stage-gated. This allows regular monthly checkpoints to learn how the innovation is evolving, how many or how much resource is it requiring, what the continued customer sentiment is, what the setbacks have been, and how you are overcoming them. This helps us to avoid those slow-moving train wrecks. The goal is to have adequate funding to see an idea through from prototype to launch.

Ranking our innovations also helps us to decide how much funding we want to designate for each.

There are three types of innovations you should have in your portfolio: transformative, breakthrough, and disruptive.

Transformative—Innovation within an existing product. In keeping with our Apple example, this is about incremental changes. This would be like going from iPhone 13 to 14 within the iPhone product line.

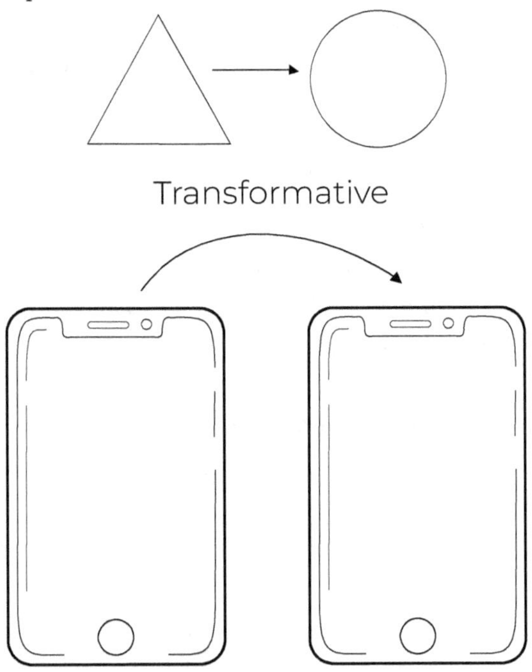

Breakthrough—Innovation within your company. By introducing the first iPad in 2010, Apple created not only a new product line but also a new consumer category of products.

Disruptive—Innovation within an industry. The Apple Watch is a step-change replacement for how you communicate, listen to music, record your workouts, and even exchange money.

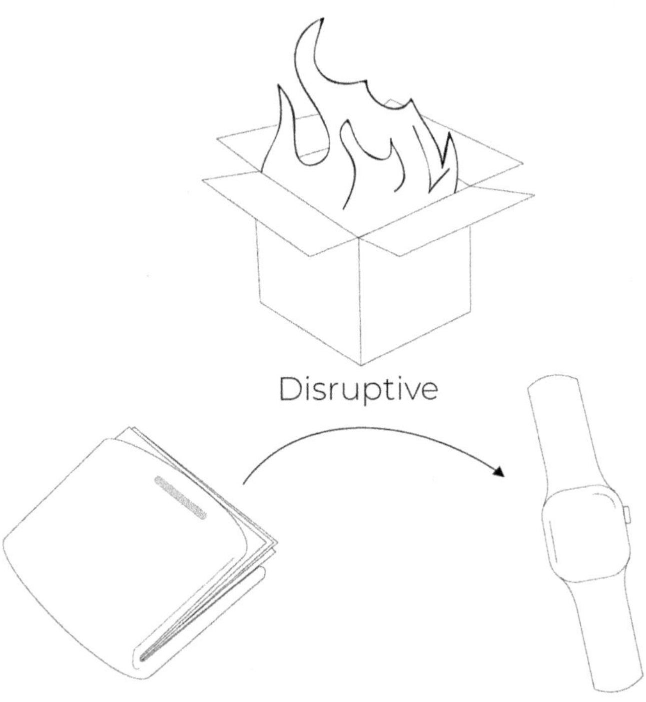

Many of the companies I work with are only thinking about transformative innovation, but to truly innovate, we need to consider all three as critical to moving your business forward and budget for all three types.

Innovation Must be Tied to ROI

When you are first innovating, ROI may begin with customer interest. It can quickly turn into customer urgency if they start to want your product. Eventually, though, it has to turn into their willingness to use or buy the product.

Before you ever build anything, those indications can be there on a smaller scale.

- Let's validate the value proposition—Why does this matter?
- Let's validate the product—What does it do to make your life better, easier, or more meaningful?

Nokia fixated on maintaining its leadership in the low-end phone business, and it missed the market coming right behind it: the rise of the smartphone. They missed key signals from the market.

In the industry I was in, as they were rebuilding this massive system that harnessed their business, all requirements faced internally, and no one was talking to end users or customers. Part of what customers will help you understand is where the market is headed, not just where it is today. Diversifying your innovation portfolio is all about getting as many people to the table as you can. At the top of that list is the customer.

Innovation Has Collaboration Opportunities

Part of what Apple did during that time was not just create the iPhone but a platform, known as the app store, for others to develop and market on. What's brilliant is as of 2023, there were almost two million apps in the app store, further tying more people to their brand and creating brand loyalty. When Apple builds something, they think of the entire ecosystem—not just the small part that they play. In doing so, they create the foundation and the systems and turn the ecosystem on its head. Whatever you do, don't create and build in a silo. Look up, look out, read the market, and build things that are not just about today but about seeing the future.

Look Back, Look Out, Look Up

The project our company was working on needed to do three things. Participants needed to look back at why it wasn't working. They just kept trying to move forward, but sometimes we need to pause to really understand why something isn't working. We needed to look out, invite our customers to the table to be a part of the conversation, and look up to understand where the market was going, not where it already was. We needed to create the environment we wanted to win.

We didn't think about how to disrupt the current landscape. You can be guaranteed our competitors were thinking about it. They were bringing solutions to the table that we couldn't dream of because we were solving the wrong problems. We were asking, *How do we get off of our old technology stack and onto a newer platform that is more stable?* The real questions to ask would have been, *How do we create the right outcomes and conditions in the market to drive the most customer value? What ideas, technology stacks, and solutions drive toward that value?*

Now, how do we, in the process, set up the right conditions to drive the market toward the future we want to create? What problems can we begin to solve today by becoming a futurist, placing a bet on tomorrow?

At the core, to fund innovation, we must understand the following:

- Innovation is freedom in the framework. Fund what matters and fund it well (but create frameworks and stage-gates to ensure our projects are on track).
- Innovation must be tied to ROI. Pull the plug early if you are not getting any ROI—no slow-moving train wrecks.
- Diversify your innovation portfolio, and plan for it. Creating the future is your survival. Don't pull from it when it gets inconvenient.

TAKE ACTION:

- What could freedom in a framework look like for your organization?
- How can your organization think differently about funding innovation?
- Which one of the three buckets do most of your innovations sit in?

FRAMEWORK:

- 3 Types of Innovation

Chapter 10
POSITION YOUR PRODUCT AND LAUNCH LIKE A PRO

"Without a community, you are simply a commodity."

SANGRAM VAJRE[37]

One time, I was brought in to launch a product no one wanted. The developers had spent months working on it, yet there was no value proposition for why anyone would buy it. We ended up scrapping a great deal of it after speaking to customers and realizing we were fighting a losing battle.

A C-level executive had an idea, and off they went building it with no questions asked. Every time I would speak to the customer, NOTHING we were building made sense to the end user. It took another year to build what people wanted and fully release

37Sangram Vajre, Twitter post, November 2020, 8:31 p.m., https://twitter.com/sangramvajre/status/1330685296682430465.

all its functionality to the market. The first thing we did was start releasing a little value at a time and getting feedback. That allowed us to tweak what we were building along the way. That team learned a hard lesson: every "good idea" is not one that should be taken to market with no questions asked.

Now that you've verified your product is desirable to the market, it's time to define the strategies and programs that will generate awareness and leads for the product. Start by defining specific plans (both internal and external) and budgets for selling products and services. Begin by asking questions: *What will extend customer loyalty? What will ensure referrals? What will allow for easy upsell?*

In order to really answer these questions, you need to be in front of your customers constantly, verifying your hypothesis. They are the best temperature check for anything you are trying to build. And remember. Not asking them is like putting your ladder against the wrong building or, worse, building the wrong building in the wrong location.

When it comes to a product launch, create a checklist to help you think of each part. For example, here's a checklist I built for a software product launch.

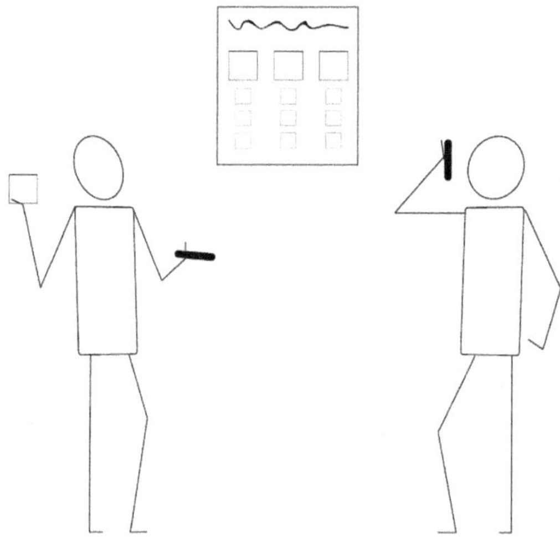

PRODUCT LAUNCH CHECKLIST

INTERNAL

- Build a cross-functional launch team.
- Schedule an internal product launch kickoff meeting. (Include a cross-functional team).
- Meet weekly to ensure your product's readiness.
- Establish a customer board to run launch ideas by to ensure your message resonates with your audience.
- Receive a go-no-go score from all involved departments. (Wait to launch if there are red flags.)
- Create internal announcements and develop training.
- Document any handoffs and key processes, and select product and process owners.

- Establish product pricing with proper margins.
- Ensure that the product is set up in all the proper internal and financial billing systems.
- Establish success metrics and reporting before launch (based on scorecards).

EXTERNAL

- Produce marketing tools like pitch decks for sales teams, press releases, external announcements, and a social media plan.
- Formulate a social media campaign and cadence calendar.
- Schedule podcast appearances.
- Write blogs about the product and the impact it's having on the market and customers.

Testimonials

There's a lot you can do to make huge waves when your product launches. I once created a launch plan for a company, complete with a story to explain how people had gotten value from the product. It implemented both images and explanations.

Whenever we launched new products, we would always talk to between three and five of our best clients, ask them to use the product in advance, provide feedback along the way, and then agree to provide us with testimonials and case studies. Some of these customers would even be willing to be references to others looking to buy. Launching a product with raving fans is *the way* to begin a product launch.

Marketing Cadences

Just as sales has a cadence for engaging their customer in the sales cycle, marketing should have a cadence to the way they release the content. Create schedules for your campaigns and the type of content and stories you'll need in advance. Provide a discount or additional products for customers who are willing to go on camera and talk about the product.

Jan 1 - 7

Sunday Jan 1	Monday Jan 2	Tuesday Jan 3	Wednesday Jan 4	Thursday Jan 5	Friday Jan 6	Saturday Jan 7
Introduction to Product A	Customer Testimonial for Product A	Customer Quote for Product A	Quote from CEO about Product A	Video Clip from CEO on Podcast	Advertising Linkedin Live with Industry Experts	Customer Testimonial for Product A

Example Content Release Plan

Weeks 1-4: Create awareness for what your product is and why it's needed.

- What is it?
- How does it work?
- How will it change their life?
- Why should they listen?

Weeks 5-8: Launch testimonials with key customers of influence.

- Video
- Quotes
- Case Studies
- Blogs

Link all your content back to a place where people can take immediate action when interested in buying.

Weeks 9-12: Elaborate on pains and gains.

- What made us decide to change?
- What will they gain by changing?

Spend time showing customers their pains. Show them why your product solves them with the gains or benefits they will receive after the fact. Pains and gains are a great way to help people connect quickly with what the product does.

Thought Leadership Roundtables

I have found the best way to get people interested in a product is to bring them together in exclusive thought leadership roundtables with other customers of the same stature. Bring all CEOs, CMOs, or CIOs together at one time to hear this product pitched, and ask them to discuss some key questions in their own groups. Later, ask them to discuss these ideas with the larger audience. This works nicely with a group of between fifteen and thirty people. Typically, we invite a few C-levels we know to bring their friends, prospects, and potential customers to the table. Therefore, you have fans and buyers in the room.

The beauty of marketing is that it's responsive. In that way, you have the chance to be iterative with your message. While there is a ton of planning that goes into it, you also need to be able to turn on a dime and adjust any messaging that is not working or resonating with your audience. Spend some time in thought leadership roundtables getting your message right. If it's not resonating there, it will not resonate with the larger audience. Create your value proposition, and pitch it until it resonates. Then, create your content from that foundation.

LAUNCH THE PRODUCT

Now it's time to officially launch. This should come with much fanfare—both internally and externally. Ensure your employees and team know about this product and can answer important questions.

Get on podcasts to talk about your innovation, send out a press release, get quotes from key customers that can be shared on social media, and blog about this product. It should not launch silently. Really put together and budget for an end-to-end campaign that makes noise and disrupts the market.

You've got this! So, remember: Don't just get out of the box. Break the box, and set it on fire. Let's go transform something!

TAKE ACTION:

- What can you begin to build now as you think about your product launch?
- How do you want your product to land in the market?
- How are you leveraging key customers to help you have a strong product launch?

AUTHOR BIO

Natalie Born is from Atlanta, Georgia. She is an innovation facilitator, consultant, author, keynote speaker, and the Host of the *Innovation Meets Leadership* Podcast. Prior to founding *Innovation Meets Leadership*, Natalie held roles as a Vice President of Innovation and Senior Vice President of Business Development.

Natalie has collaborated on two approved US patents and has over fifteen years of experience leading product development, UI/UX, web development, and strategy and marketing teams. Natalie has worked with organizations such as Career Builder, First Data, IHG, and ADP, and led major initiatives in over eighteen countries.

Natalie is married to Aaron and they have two daughters.

Follow Natalie @innovationmeetsleadership on Instagram, Facebook, or Linkedin, or head over to www.innovationmeetsleadership.com for more innovation resources.

THE AVAIL PODCAST

HOSTED BY VIRGIL SIERRA

www.ingramcontent.com/pod-product-compliance
Lightning Source LLC
LaVergne TN
LVHW010700110826
845149LV00014B/3180

9781960678225